People of Legend

NATIVE AMERICANS OF THE SOUTHWEST
People of Legend

PHOTOGRAPHS AND TEXT BY
John Annerino

SIERRA CLUB BOOKS · SAN FRANCISCO

The Sierra Club, founded in 1892 by John Muir, has devoted itself to the study and protection of the earth's scenic and ecological resources—mountains, wetlands, woodlands, wild shores and rivers, deserts and plains. The publishing program of the Sierra Club offers books to the public as a nonprofit educational service in the hope that they may enlarge the public's understanding of the Club's basic concerns. The point of view expressed in each book, however, does not necessarily represent that of the Club. The Sierra Club has some sixty chapters coast to coast, in Canada, Hawaii, and Alaska. For information about how you may participate in its programs to preserve wilderness and the quality of life, please address inquiries to Sierra Club, 730 Polk Street, San Francisco, CA 94109.

COVER: Yavapai bullfighter and rodeo clown Arleigh Banaha

FRONTISPIECE: Young *fariseos,* "pharisees," wear sacred white clay highlighted with charcoal. (Sonora, Mexico)

LIBRARY OF CONGRESS CATALOGING-IN-PUBLICATION DATA

Annerino, John.
    People of legend : Native Americans of the Southwest / photographs and text by John Annerino.
        p.   cm.
    Includes bibliographical references.
    ISBN: 0-87156-433-5 (alk. paper)
    1. Indians of North America — Southwest, New.   2. Indians of North America — Southwest, New — Pictorial works.   I. Title.
E78.S7A65 1996
979′.00497—dc20   96-8132
                                                                                          CIP

Production by Janet Vail and Robin Rockey
Jacket design by Paula Schlosser
Book design by Paula Schlosser
Map by Hilda Chen
Chapter motifs by Rob Badger and Nita Winter

Printed in Singapore

10 9 8 7 6 5 4 3 2 1

For Chico Shuni, who held his ground to the last man.
And for my love, Alejandrina.

CONTENTS

ACKNOWLEDGMENTS

I'D LIKE TO THANK the many Native Americans who selflessly shared their dreams, customs, and ceremonies with me.

Among the *Nde*/Apache: Sterling Goseyun, Juliette Goseyun, Armando D. Goseyun, Sheena Marie Goseyun, Terry and Lorraine Rodríguez, Mrs. Robert Duncan, medicine man Leroy Kenton, Harrison Bonito, Cynthia Hinton, medicine man Robertson Preston, Mrs. Robertson Preston, Rodela Smith, Wanda Smith, and Mr. and Mrs. Christopher Duncan.

Among the *O'ob*/Mountain Pima: *curandero* Luis Coyote, Rosa Galaviz, Lidia Castellano, José Angel Contreras Sierra, *gobenador* Romelia Alvárez Arena, *gobenador* José Manuel Galaviz Lao, Candelaria Moreno Valentín and Luis Romero, Juanita Sierra Lao, Edgardo Bojorquez Cosme, José de Jesús Miramón González, Francisco Carillo Loya, Hernán and Felix Rodríguez Sierra, Pedro Lao Negrete, *sobador* Cristóbal Galaviz López, *curandera* Cruzita Lao Rodríguez, capitán Juan Ramón Rodríguez Galaviz, elder Juan Rodríguez, padre Davíd José Beaumont OFM Cap, and translator and friend Bertha Alicia Aguilar Valenzuela.

Among the *Tohono O'odham*/Pápago: George Francisco, Stella Tucker, Wade Escalante, Zack Ortega, Shelton Escalante, Elvino Valisto, Denise Martínez, Ed Kisto, Oscar Velasco León and family, Eugenio Velasco Ortega and Herlinda León Pacheco, Rod Treviño Velasco, Rafaél García, Raymundo Montejo Robles, and Verna Morrow; and *Hia Ced O'odham*/Sand Pápago Chico Shuni.

Among the *Akimel O'odham*/Pima: Bruce Marietta, Adrienne and Danielle Enos, Barnaby Lewis, Gwendolyn Paul, Noline Jackson, and the Basket dancers; *Pi:pa:s*/Maricopa Ronald Mack; *Kwaca:n*/Quechan Roland Golding and son, and the Bird dancers and singers; *Makháv*/Mojave Valerie Welch, Iva R. McCord, Donna L. Stanley and the Bird dancers; *Hwalapay*/Hualapai Delbert Havatone, Archie Matuck, Jessica Powskey, Scott Crozier, and Michael Vaughn; *Havasuwa ∂pa*/Havasupai Denny Wescogame, Kirby Suathojame, Ray Kaska; *Pac∂*/ Yavapai Arleigh Banaha; and Shoshoni Brad Díaz.

Among the *Diné*/Navajo: Richie Anderson, Marvin Hardy, Liana Lynn Cleveland, Candice John, Elsie Plummer, James A. Kimble, Marie H. Belone, Aisha Oldham, Josephine Tracy, Raymond Haskie and family, Alfred James, Anderson Haskie, Mr. and Mrs. Harrison Nez, T.K. Whitman, George Etsitty, Bruce Lee Jackson, and Stu and Flo Barton.

Among the *Ohken*/San Juan Tewa: Robert Aquino, Joseph Martínez and Joseph Martínez, Jr., Max Ortíz, Jr., Wilbert Cruz, Jr., Janet "Corn" Martínez, Johnna Aquino, and the One-Horned Buffalo dancers; *Siwi*/Zuni, Ashleigh B. Yamutewa, Joy L. Edaake, the Zuni Olla Maidens, Fernando Cellición and the Traditional Zuni Dancers, Sylvin

Noche, Alton Nastacio, DuWayne Panteal, and Carmela Cellición; San Fidel Pueblo, Bellamino, Carmen Key-ope, Paul Enciso, Jonathan García, Sunrise Enciso, David García, Amoré Enciso, Amura Enciso, Erin Juanico, Ben García, Michael García; and Weimunuche band of Southern Ute Norman "Buffalo" Lansing.

I'd also like to thank: Stephanie Robertson, Elvira Mendoza, Esther Meyer, Bill Broyles, John Dell, Neil Carmony, Ida B. Annerino, Deana Jackson-Brown, John Bilby, David Spinner, Tony Ebarb, Julie Murphy, Sandy Lanham, Noëlle Byloos and the InterTribal Ceremonial. And I'd especially like to thank retired *Life* picture editor Melvin L. Scott for his encouragement throughout the many stages of this book and for his keen eye on helping me cut and edit the photography.

INTRODUCTION

We have lived upon this land from days
beyond history's records, far past any
living memory, deep into the time of
legend. The story of my people and the
story of this place are one single
story. No man can think of us without
also thinking of this place. We are
always joined together.

Taos Pueblo elder

Nowhere else in north america is the landscape on such a grand and spectacular scale as in the Southwest, and nowhere else does such a large concentration of aboriginal Americans maintain their traditional lifeways and spiritual beliefs as in the mythical heartland of Native America. It is here that the supernal crests of the southern Rocky Mountains form the backbone of this great continent where, on their cloud-capped western front, they give way to the soaring monoliths and red sandstone mesas of the mile-high Colorado Plateau. Here the deep, timeless labyrinth of canyons and fissures formed by the Colorado River and its tributaries cuts through the black lava crust of the Sonoran desert and empties its sands into the mesmerizing seas of the California Gulf. The fact that a large diversity of indigenous peoples thrived in the Southwest relatively unscathed until the last century had as much to do with their isolation as it did with these magnificent landforms, which proved nearly impenetrable to outsiders.

The journey for the first Americans to reach the Southwest was a long and treacherous one. Anthropologists tell us it began about 50,000 B.C., when the continent's first wave of immigrants crossed the Siberian land bridge and traveled the length of the Rocky Mountains, hunting woolly mammoths with little more than flimsy spears. Their descendants, cunning hunters and gatherers, dispersed throughout the Southwest circa 10,000 B.C., and they comprised a handful of distinct cultures that were molded by the awesome landforms they inhabited.

Foremost among these ancient peoples, perhaps, were the *anaasází*, "enemy ancestors," who settled throughout the burnished escarpments of the Four Corners region of the Colorado Plateau. They constructed spectacular pueblos like Cliff Palace at Mesa Verde and they built great ceremonial kivas at Chaco Canyon that were linked to distant settlements by an elaborate network of trails. The Anasazi farmed the depths of the Grand Canyon near the roaring Colorado River in the spring and stalked the aspen groves of the North Rim for deer in the fall. And then, about A.D. 1200, they vanished. No one knows why. Some say drought; others speculate that a burgeoning populace outstripped the natural carrying capacity of the land and its water sources; and still others argue that the Anasazi were driven out by Shoshoni raiders from the north or by large bands of Athapaskans who migrated into their lands. Yet others claim that the Anasazi never disappeared but merely regrouped, retreated to the protection of their high mesas, and evolved into the Pueblo peoples of New Mexico and Arizona.

A sketch of the prehistory of the Southwest would include several other distinct cultural groups. The largest among them was thought to be the Hohokam, who might have

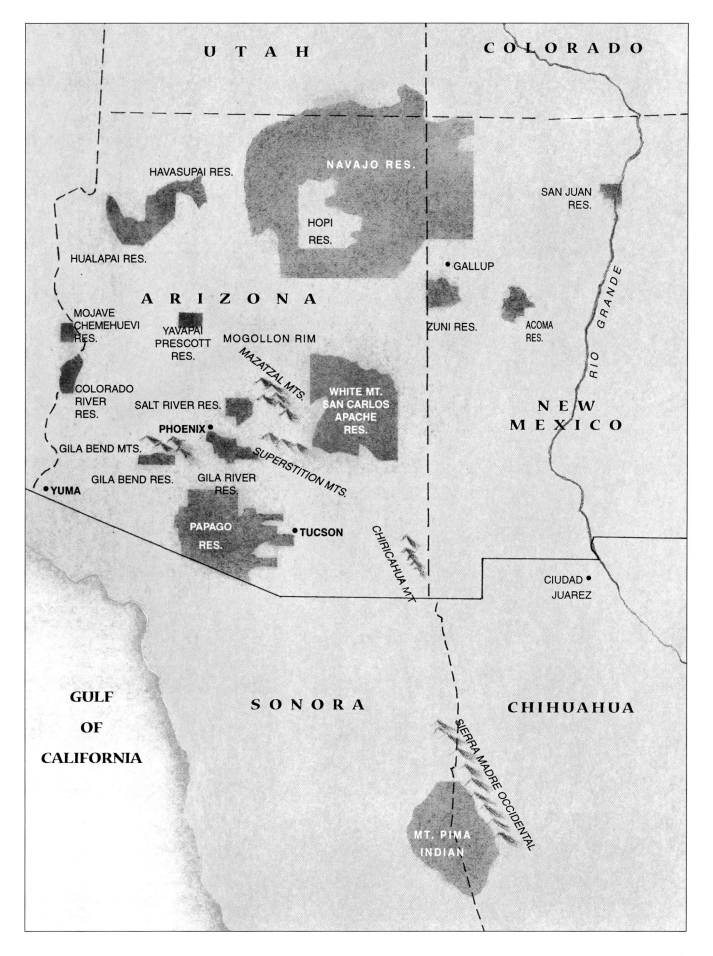

numbered 100,000 at the height of their civilization. In the Piman language their name means "those who have gone." The Hohokam were no less adaptive to their harsh environment than the Anasazi, but whereas the Anasazi built multistoried cliff dwellings, the Hohokam irrigated the Sonoran desert on a scale unparalleled in this hemisphere. Using crude wooden digging sticks, the Hohokam successfully farmed the Sonoran desert near the confluence of central Arizona's Salt and Verde rivers by digging 300 miles of canals in the stone-hard caliche and black *malpais,* "badlands." Like the Pueblo people to the north, who feel kinship to the ancestral lands of the Anasazi, traditional Pima also trace their cultural rhythms back to the Hohokam, who inexplicably departed from the area about A.D. 1400.

Follow the ancient tracks northwest from the Hohokam and you will enter the stark realm of the Patayan people; they were forced to become nomadic hunters and gatherers simply because they roamed the driest and most forbidding reaches of the Sonoran desert in west-central Arizona. It was a desperate fringe of empty ground that offered little more than scant rainfall for floodwater agriculture; blistering creosote flats for gathering mesquite beans, saguaro, and prickly pear fruit; and craggy desert sierras for tracking bighorn sheep. Whether modern Yuman-speaking tribes such as the Yavapai, Hualapai, and Mojave had direct cultural links to the Patayan is still debated, but they moved into the ancestral grounds of the Patayan about A.D. 1400.

Linking the Patayan homeland on the west with that of the Mogollon people to the east is the Mogollon Rim, a pine-covered precipice that arcs across Arizona and disappears near the border highlands of New Mexico. Here, the Mogollon people tilled corn, which was first carried north from Mesoamerica about 3000 B.C., as well as beans and squash. They hunted deer and bison with spears called *atlatls.* Creation myths, as well as ethnographic reports, however, provide few cultural links between the disappearance of the Mogollon people about A.D. 1000 and the arrival of the Western and Chiricahua Apache in the area four centuries later.

As a region, the Southwest is as much a state of mind as a geographical place. Where it begins and where it ends are questions that have persisted from the days of nineteenth-century boundary surveyors who used neat lines to divide rugged landforms; modern writers have tried to trace its cultural landscape with their pens. For our purposes, the Southwest encompasses an eight-state region of the United States and Mexico; it extends from Las Vegas, Nevada, east to Las Vegas, New Mexico, and from Durango, Colorado, south to Durango, Mexico. I've included this vast region in the book except in its southern terminus, which I've limited to the northern Sierra Madre of Sonora and Chihuahua. Fifty indigenous groups still live within this area, and to photograph and describe them all is a task far beyond the scope of this book. Thus, I limited my selection to six principal groupings, based primarily on the diversity of the physiographic provinces the people inhabit.

Headwaters of the Río Mayo, Basaseáchic Falls forms a spectacular landmark that divides the ancestral land of the O'ob from that of the neighboring Tarahumara in Chihuahua, Mexico.

In southeastern Arizona, you will visit the "People of the Mountains," the Western Apache; they have lived within view of their sacred mountains since about A.D. 1400. Two hundred miles south live the "People of the Sierra," the O'ob; they have inhabited the Continental Divide region of the northern Sierra Madre Occidental since before Spanish missionaries first attempted to convert them during the seventeenth century.

Some linguists suggest the ancient O'ob are really the ancestors to the "People of the Desert," the Pápago; they have survived in the harshest tract of the Sonoran desert of northwest Sonora and southwest Arizona since the Hohokam era. So have the "People of the River," the Pima; they inhabit central Arizona's Salt and Verde river valley region to the north. Linguistic cousins to the Pápago, the Pima are linked to distant river-dwelling peoples like the Mojave and Hualapai by the pulse of the Gila and Colorado rivers; the Mojave inhabit the desert region of the lower Colorado River, and the Hualapai inhabit the western Grand Canyon. Together, their lands formed the vast ancestral region once inhabited by the Patayan. Atop the Colorado Plateau you will visit the "People of the Mesas," the Navajo; they have lived within the sacred realm of *dinétah,* "the land," since about A.D. 1500.

At the end of this cultural odyssey, you will visit Pueblo peoples such as the Zuni, Keresan, and Tewa; they still inhabit the mesa and river valleys abandoned by the Anasazi. Here, in the redrock country of New Mexico, indigenous peoples like the Totonaca and Aztec come from as far away as central Mexico to join the Northern and Southern Plains Indians and the Pueblo peoples in the largest traditional Gathering of Nations in the Southwest.

The journey for these Native Americans to reach this point in history, however, has been filled with tragedy and despair. No matter how well they adapted to the Southwest's environmental extremes, they were not prepared for the insidious forces that challenged their existence during the nineteenth century. When the first waves of European immigrants came west across the continent with dreams of Manifest Destiny, several pivotal events that took place on the periphery of the Southwest shaped the destiny of those Native Americans living within it.

Gold discovered in 1848 at Sutter's Mill in California's Sierra Nevada started the gold rush; within ten years, two-thirds of an estimated 150,000 California Indians had been annihilated. Then the Homestead Act of 1862 started a stampede for land that was disastrous for Native Americans. Devastating epidemics followed the settlers, and massacres like Bear River (Utah), Sand Creek (Colorado), and Wounded Knee Creek (South Dakota) followed the soldiers sent to protect both the settlers and the forty-niners. In spite of winning decisive battles such as Little Bighorn, Native America could not win the war in the face of such overwhelming odds.

Arizona, too, earned an unconscionable reputation for the wanton massacres of the Kewevkapaya Yavapai at Skeleton Cave and the Aravaipa Apache at Camp Grant. Yet these grim legacies foreshadowed the Navajo's own epic tragedy during their bitter Long Walk in the winter of 1864. Faced with the scorched-earth campaign of Brigadier General James H. Carleton and Kit Carson, 3,945 starving Navajos were forced to trek 300 grueling miles from Fort Defiance, Arizona, to Bosque Redondo, New Mexico. Only an act of Congress, ratified four years later, could free all 9,022 Navajos imprisoned there and return them to their homeland.

Not all Native Americans were as successful as the Navajo in reclaiming their tribal territories. But the long trail of broken treaties that followed could not crush the Native American spirit, any more than the government's shameful policy of dislocation, assimilation, reservation, and termination could force them to relinquish their identity, even after their population was reduced to 250,000 by 1910 from the estimated 5 to 10 million Native Americans who inhabited the continent before Columbus "discovered" it.

Indeed, modern Native America has not escaped the crime, gangs, drugs, alcohol, unemployment, and poverty that have beset Americans everywhere. But something noble and something beautiful has survived the history of injustice, turmoil, and despair. That is the focus of this book.

It was here in the mythic Southwest, where time falls away, where Native peoples hold open the door to America's aboriginal past, and where ancestral lands give birth to sacred visions, that I first went looking for Native America.

Navajo perform Plains Indian-style dances in downtown Gallup, New Mexico.

The seed for this lifelong journey took hold years ago, when I fled the miasma of Phoenix for the tranquillity of the nearby Superstition Mountains; in the spring of youth, I had repeatedly ventured on foot into the haunting interior of these mountains in quest of my own spirit. But it wasn't until much later that I learned *Kakatak Tamai,* "Crooked-Top Mountain," was the center of Pima legend; the legend starts like this:

From the Superstition mountain rose the eagle;
From the sluggish moving Gila rose the hawk ...
There I am running, there I am running.
The Shadow of Crooked Mountain.

Throughout my life, the journey toward this book continued. Every region I explored—whether I was teaching survival to non-Indians in an austere tract of the Eagletail Mountains or guiding young Navajos along their ancient paths to Rainbow Bridge—the questions always persisted: Who had lived here? How had they survived? How had they viewed these spectacular landforms? And what had become of these people?

I traveled in many directions, on long journeys—sometimes to the far ends of the Southwest, other times into its remotest reaches—before I began to answer those basic questions. For five years I retraced the ancient Hopi, Havasupai, and Mojave trade routes by running hundreds of miles at a time on desert paths through the Grand Canyon, northern Arizona, and California's Mojave Desert, as ancient traders had done. But that initiation led to an even longer spirit quest, which culminated in a month-long 750-mile run along ancient trails and routes from Mexico to Utah.

As I was shivering around my small bivouac fires, a second set of questions haunted me: Where were these Native Americans today? What traditions had they kept alive? And what ceremonies were they still performing? So my lifelong quest brought me back to the beginning of the cultural circle, but this time the path led me to the foot of a maze inhabited by fifty indigenous groups that fortunately still survive in the Southwest.

Among them are the Tarahumara, who inhabit the Sierra Madre Occidental of Chihuahua, Mexico. My formative visit among them changed forever the way I had been taught to embrace the European concept of wilderness and "Indian Country" to the north. Here, in the Barranca del Cobre region of the Sierra Madre, 50,000 Tarahumara were still living on their ancestral lands. At a remote pueblo in the heart of the Sierra Madre, I watched and photographed in awe as hundreds of Tarahumara gathered to celebrate their sacred *tutúburi* ceremonies, much the way they had for centuries. The rhythmic echoes of beating drums and the fleeting shadows dancing in the yellow glow of a dozen fires throughout the cold starry nights mesmerized me. Upon my return to Arizona, I no longer viewed our national parks, wilderness areas, and wildlife preserves as "natural" because, in most instances, they lacked the one component that would make them ecologically complete: the indigenous peoples who had been displaced to create them.

In many respects, this book is the answer to my first questions. Traditional Native Americans believe in the sanctity of the four cardinal directions. And I, too, believed that they would shape my journey. I didn't know in which direction this journey would end, but I did know where I wanted it to begin: in the east, with the Apache. No tribe had earned a more fearful reputation in the Southwest—oftentimes with no basis in fact—than these fleet-footed guerrilla fighters. Yet for me it was a fortuitous beginning, because no one treated me more openly—as rapidly—as the Apache. And no other non-Indians I've met in my life have spoken with me about love as freely as the Apache elders did. Thus, at the end of my first stay in their ceremonial encampment, I was beside myself about how I could possibly thank them for sharing such a sacred aspect of their culture with me, other than to say I would send photographs, as I always do. And do you know what they did? The Apache people thanked me for sharing their culture with them!

Today, near their holy shrines in the alpine forests of the Piñaleno Mountains, black-masked *ga'an,* "mountain spirits," still dance throughout the night to carry the sacred prayers of the Apache. In the rugged forests of the Sierra Madre, the O'ob still hear the haunting wails of the *onza,* their mythical wildcat. In the vast sweep of the Sonoran desert, the Pápago still play the ancient stickball game of *toka.* In the alluring depths of the Grand Canyon, the Hualapai still run the turbulent waters of the Colorado River first navigated on reed *balsas* by their ancestors. On the cusp of the Colorado Plateau, the Navajo still revere the sacred mountains that mark their hallowed ground. And in the ancient settlements overlooking the Zuni River and the upper Río Grande, the Pueblo people still celebrate the buffalo dance in reverence to its great spirit.

I now invite you to turn the page and share the rich heritage Native Americans shared with me.

PEOPLE OF THE *Mountains*

Apache / *Nde*

We are vanishing from the earth,
yet I cannot think we are useless
or Usen would not have created us.

GERONIMO

CLIMB THE TANGLED RIDGES of the Pinaleño Mountains in southeastern Arizona and you will see there is no end to the world the Apache god Usen created for the Nde. To the north is the 11,420-foot *Dzil Ligai*, "White Mountain," the sacred mountain of the White Mountain Apache; its holy waters carved the two-hundred-mile-long Colorado River Gorge. To the east are *Pinos Altos*, the "Tall Pines," of New Mexico; the birthplace of Geronimo, this area forms the headwaters of the Gila River. To the west are the rugged flanks of the Galiuro and Santa Catalina mountains; they form the lush riparian corridor for the San Pedro River. And to the south are the wind-sculpted ramparts of the Dragoon Mountains; they shroud the hidden tomb of Cochise and the spirit trails of Geronimo.

The Nde were Southern Athapaskans who migrated from the Mackenzie River Basin of Canada about 3,500 years ago. Why the Nde left the subarctic cordillera, which they followed south along the Continental Divide, or how long the 2,000-mile migration took cannot be said with any certainty. But once the Nde arrived in the Southwest between A.D. 1000 and 1500, they dispersed into seven Apachean-speaking tribes.

They are still known as the Jicarilla, Lipan, Mescalero, Kiowa-Apache, Navajo (shortened from the Spanish *Apache de Nabajó*), Chiricahua, and Western Apache. During the Nde's reign, however, they controlled a tribal territory comprising some 90,000 square miles, ranging from the western plains of Oklahoma to the White Mountains of Arizona, and from the southern escarpment of the Colorado Rockies deep into the Sierra Madre of Mexico. Adapting to a region of mountains fleeced with powdered snow, wild canyons haunted with daylong shadows, and deserts heated by a white sun, each tribe subdivided further into smaller bands and sub-bands, many of them taking Nde names that described the environment they inhabited.

The Apache creation myth we know from shaman Palmer Valor. Valor was born to the *tɫ́·slednt`i·dn* clan, and before his death in Bylas, Arizona, in 1930 the 96-year-old shaman told Grenville Goodwin the story "When the Earth Was Made." In the beginning, the shaman explained through his interpreter, there were only four people, and "they set up" the earth. But it was so windy, the shaman continued, the earth blew off. So a black cane covered with black metal thorns was used to hold down the east. A blue cane with blue metal thorns was used to hold down the south. A yellow cane with yellow metal thorns was used to hold down the west. And a white cane covered with white metal thorns held down the north. The shaman said the earth was cold, so they kept it warm by giving it "hair," in the form of trees. But it was still weak, so they gave it "bones," in the form of mountains. And when it needed to breathe, they gave

Cynthia Hinton in a traditional camp dress.
(Bylas, Arizona)

it thunder and lightning, from which water was born. The shaman also told Goodwin, "They made the sun so it traveled close over the earth from east to west." But it was too hot, so they moved the sun back. And then they made the moon to track through the night. Wild fruit and food began to grow. They became a people. And then everything was just right.

Conquistador Francisco Vásquez de Coronado rode north out of Mexico into the world of the Nde in 1540; he was searching for Cíbola, the fabled seven cities of the gold where "women wore strings of gold beads, and the men girdles of gold."

It was not the last such tale of riches to lure the White Eyes into the heartland of the Nde. Three centuries later, Nde scouts saw prairie schooners of eastern settlers rolling west in quest of gold, God, or California. President James K. Polk, inspired by the words of politician William Gilpin, called this heady spirit of expansionism "manifest destiny." For many Native Americans it was the beginning of a catastrophe.

The world of the Nde changed. Deer, bear, elk, and antelope fell to the rapacious muzzle blasts of settlers' .44–.40 caliber, lever-action rifles. Hunting the depleted game herds with bows and arrows became even more difficult. Food sources such as juniper berries, piñon nuts, and roasted mescal hearts were not enough to sustain the Nde, especially when they were driven off ancestral lands that the settlers, miners, and cattlemen staked as their own. The Nde developed a tactical culture of raiding and guerrilla warfare, but it was a level of warfare the Nde could not sustain. They were massacred at places like Aravaipa Creek, where on April 28, 1871, six Anglos, forty-eight Mexican-Americans, and ninety-four Pápagos from Tucson murdered 108 defenseless old men, women, and children and even slaughtered the camp dogs. Scalping at the hands of bounty hunters was commonplace; Sonora and Chihuahua were offering a hundred pesos for each male Apache scalp. Geronimo and thirty-eight Chiricahua Apache fled south with 5,000 American troops in pursuit.

Creation Myth of the Apache

— · — · — · — · — · —

*I*N THE BEGINNING there were only four people, and they set up the earth. But it was so windy the earth blew off. So a black cane covered with black metal thorns was used to hold down the east. A blue cane with blue metal thorns was used to hold down the south. A yellow cane with yellow metal thorns was used to hold down the west. And a white cane covered with white metal thorns held down the north. The earth was cold, so they kept it warm by giving it hair in the form of trees.

Geronimo held out in the northern Sierra Madre until hunger and fatigue finally drove him to surrender at Cañon de los Embudos, Sonora, on September 3, 1886. The Nde feared total annihilation, and so they continued to seek *di yih,* "supernatural power," in their ceremonies. Other Native peoples in Arizona, such as the Havasupai and Kaibab Paiute, adopted the Ghost Dance of the Sioux to ward off the White Eyes. But the Nde abided by the most sacred of their ceremonies, the puberty rite of *na ih es,* "getting her ready."

Fortunately, *na ih es* survives today, as do the seven original Apachean-speaking tribes who inhabit lands in Oklahoma, New Mexico, Colorado, Utah, and Arizona. I witnessed *na ih es* among the San Carlos Apache, one of the Western Apache's five principal bands. (The others are the Northern Tonto, Southern Tonto, Cibecue, and White Mountain Apache.) They live throughout eastern and central Arizona and today depend on cattle ranching, lumber, tourism, and gaming for economic survival. They also depend on their sacred mountains and ceremonies for spiritual renewal.

Helped by a friend, Wanda Smith (wearing white buckskins) takes a break during the four-day-and-night ceremony. (Arizona)

Towering high above the ancestral land of the Nde is 10,720-foot *Dzil nchaa si an,* Mount Graham; it is the sacred mountain of the San Carlos Apache and the place of many of their prayers. One goes like this:

The living sky black-spotted.
The living sky blue-spotted.
The living sky yellow-spotted.
The living sky white-spotted.

The Nde still live at the foot of this holy mountain and still see in the living sky yellow-spotted a great ancient vision of Apache religious life: White Shell Woman.

She has been dancing there since the dawn of man, and she will still be dancing there when living sky black-spotted comes. The days and nights will come and go, and she will still face east to be impregnated by the morning sun. She is *ih sta nedleheh,* the mother of proud children. They are the Nde "[Apache] people," and they still gather to bear witness to her sacred transformation. In the ancient rite of *na ih es,* Apache girls follow this path to womanhood.

Few ceremonies I knew about at the time intrigued me more than *na ih es,* but I wasn't sure how to go about finding one. Non-Indians who had gotten wind of my travels advised me to contact a handful of scholars. I tried, but none returned my phone calls. I talked to a Tohono O'odham elder about this later, and he laughed, making a three-inch gap between his right thumb and index finger. "They get big bucks to study us Indians, and they don't want anyone sniffing around the henhouse." Indeed, the concept of Native Americans as intellectual property has existed since the reservation census figures were first compiled. The story goes that one Navajo told census takers that the average family consisted of five and a half people: a mother, father, three children, and an anthropologist.

While I was photographing the July Fourth Window Rock rodeo, a chance meeting with an Apache bull-rider led me to Bylas a week later. There, in a ceremonial encampment, I was introduced as a photojournalist to the sponsor of the ceremony, the parents, the medicine man, and everybody else within earshot. The Apache are forthright people and somebody asked me, "What do you want?" I handed them my blue notebook and let it do the talking. In it were color prints of sacred Tarahumara ceremonies I had photographed over the years. Then somebody said, "How much?" I took that to mean, "How much was I going to pay the medicine man?" Medicine men have traditionally been paid for performing ceremonies since the days blankets and horses were first traded for a curing. I explained the purpose of the book and offered to make them a portfolio of photographs they could have as their own record of the ceremony. Everybody started laughing. Then the father said, "I thought you wanted *me* to pay *you*."

It was the first Apache ceremony I would photograph; I didn't want to be obtrusive. So I looked to Mrs. Robert Duncan, the *ndeh guhyaneh,* or "respected elder," who was overseeing all aspects of this *na ih es,* and she carefully guided me throughout the ceremony.

It is being held for Sheena Goseyun. She is *sà'hndè·dò·t'án,* San Carlos Apache. She is facing east, in the direction of the rising sun, where the earth was first set up. She is dancing with a cane called *gish ih zha ha* that she will use in old age; it is adorned with eagle feathers for her protection, and with green, black, yellow, and white ribbons that represent the cardinal directions. She is helped by her *na ihł esn,* "one who prepares her," or godmother, who has made a lifelong vow to guide her through the stages of life. Together, they are guided by a *dí yin,* "one who has power," medicine man Leroy Kenton, who leads the singing of the sacred songs. The family of the sponsor, their friends, and many of the hundreds of others from the community show their reverence and reciprocal support by dancing throughout the four days and nights of the ceremony. This support is called *shi ti ke,* "my good friend," and it reaffirms the community's bond. Many have brought extra food—including meat, beans, flour, sugar, coffee, and soda—to share because two steers are not enough.

After a long day and night of dancing in the wind-blown dust and sweltering desert heat, the journey toward womanhood has only begun.

When darkness falls, black-masked *ga'an,* "mountain spirits," whirl into the midst; they are guided by their own *dí yin,* medicine man Robertson Preston, in the warding off of evil forces. Their magic shadows flicker around the billowing yellow flames of a towering bonfire as the chanting and drumming continue deep into the night. When daybreak comes, the *ga'an* resume dancing, whirling in and out of the sacred teepee; it represents Sheena's house and it is protected by eagle feathers.

On the final day Sheena appears in traditional buckskins, and the first medicine man sprinkles *hadn tin,* "sacred yellow powder," over her forehead. In this state of transformation, she receives the power of *ba koh di yi,* "she can perform miracles." She is White Shell Woman, and she in turn is blessed by the long line of Nde—including the sick and infirm—who have come to be blessed by her.

She is still facing east. The white shell dangles over her forehead. She has become the mother of her people.

And nothing is more sacred.

Or beautiful.

Except, possibly, the way several Apache elders greet me at the end of *na ih es.* They shake my hand and say, "Thank you for sharing our culture with us." Their words fill me with awe.

Respected elder, Mrs. Robert Duncan.

(Arizona)

*Women share stories and prepare frybread at a
traditional ceremonial encampment. (Arizona)*

Medicine man Robertson Preston (center, in sunglasses), drummers, singers, and the ga'an, "mountain spirits." (Arizona)

OPPOSITE: Ga'an, *"mountain spirit." (Arizona)*

White Shell Woman Wanda Smith. (Arizona)

Medicine man Leroy Kenton (in blue shirt) *sings
the sacred songs for Sheena Goseyun's
na ih es ceremony. (Arizona)*

Godmother Lorraine Rodríguez helps Sheena
Goseyun during na ih es; *she has taken a lifelong*
vow to guide her. (Arizona)

Dancing with the sacred cane that will support her in old age, Sheena Goseyun is blessed with hadn tin. *(Arizona)*

Mountain spirits dance throughout the night to
bless the sacred grounds and to carry prayers
for the Apache. (Arizona)

OPPOSITE: *Ga'an, "mountain spirits," bless Wanda*
Smith (in white buckskins) in her sacred teepee.
(Arizona)

PEOPLE OF THE *Sierra*

Mountain Pima / *O'ob*

The sun is our Father,
the moon is our Mother.

JUAN RODRÍGUEZ, O'OB ELDER

TWO HUNDRED MILES SOUTH of the Arizona border, Mexico's Sierra Madre Occidental forms the magnificent southern half of the Continental Divide and the border between Sonora and Chihuahua. Here the rivers also run to divided seas but in so doing they create vaulting cataracts that tumble from old-growth forests through deep barrancas, which give way to subtropical thornscrub. It is a land, wrote Texas folklorist J. Frank Dobie, "of primeval and aboriginal mysteries," where "no one now lives, though the territory is claimed by the Pima Indians. It belongs to deer, lobo wolves, panthers, jaguars, and other animals."

But, in fact, it also belongs to the O'ob, or Mountain Pima; their elusive habitations escaped Dobie's observations during his romantic quest for the *onza,* a mythical wildcat, seventy years ago.

Gaze north along the Continental Divide, and you will see the verdant river valleys of the Ópata. To the southwest, the Guarijío—the lost tribe of the Sierra Madre—still inhabit the deciduous gorge of the Río Mayo. To the south, beyond the distant mesas, there is no end to the indigenous people who still dwell there, among them the Tarahumara, the Tepehuán, the Cora, and the Huichol. But to the east, in the high forests and meadows, you'll find the lands of the O'ob. It is a world lost in time: here, the O'ob are still living as their ancestors did a century ago. White beans are still cooked in clay ollas in dark, smoky caves. Ceremonial mounds of hand-tossed stones still mark the sacred mesas where men once danced like deer. And long-forgotten pictographs still record the passing of the Chiricahua Apache. It is here that the forest-dwelling O'ob maintain a closeness with nature many native people of the Southwest no longer know, a relationship formed during their origin.

One version of the O'ob's creation myth was recorded, translated, and abridged thus:

"We were taught as children that the sun is our Father and that the moon is our Mother. God made the people out of clay of the earth. These first people God made were not very good; so God changed many of these people into animals we see today. The lions, rabbits, coyotes, and other animals were all people before. Then God sent a great flood to destroy all the people because they were so bad. God made people again, this time smaller than the first, but they were also very bad. So God sent the sun down close to the earth to destroy them by the heat of a great fire. Many people hid in caves to not be burn't, but they died there and that is why even today you can see mummies who died in the caves long ago. Then God made people for the third time, smaller than even the second group of people. These people were pleasing to God so he let them live."

What remains of a sacred O'ob burial cave looted by anthropologists and grave robbers in Mexico's Sierra Madre.

The handful of O'ob who lived in this third world beyond may have been visited by Europeans as early as 1540, when Alvar Núñez Cabeza de Vaca forged a tortuous path across the Sierra Madre, a remarkable journey he described in *Adventures in the Unknown Interior of America*. Some ethnographers believe it was about that time that the O'ob began migrating northwest into the parched deserts of what the Spaniards called *Pimería*

Alta, "Land of the Upper Pimas." Here, in what would become Arizona, they eked out a living and prospered culturally as the Akimel O'odham (Pima), Tohono O'odham (Pápago), and Hia Ced O'odham (Sand Pápago). Or, perhaps in the telling the migration pattern was reversed, because linguists have also linked the O'ob to the Tepehuán, who live farther south in the rugged Sierra Madre than the Tarahumara. But the Pima Bajo, "Lower Pimas," who continue to live in the Sonoran desert to the west of the O'ob, have their own beliefs about their highland cousins; they call the O'ob the *Táramil O'odham,* or the "Tarahumara-like people," for surviving in the Sierra Madre much the way the neighboring Tarahumara do.

Whatever their true origin, the O'ob were believed to number about 4,530 souls when missionaries tallied their baptisms in 1634. But it was not long before the O'ob, the Tarahumara, Yaqui, and Mayo revolted. They were perishing from strange diseases brought by the "black robes." And they didn't take to the missionaries' methods of forced labor, relocation, or conversion to Christianity. In 1697 the O'ob briefly joined forces with the neighboring Tarahumara to fight off the Spaniards. But in 1767 the indigenous people of Mexico received a reprieve from the missionaries when the Jesuits were expelled by the government.

Relic bands of O'ob held steadfast to their forested sierras, and in their oral tradition they still talk of other pivotal events that shaped their destiny; to this day, there are still whispers of the stealthy Apache. Using the Río Aros and Río Mulatos as travel corridors, the Chiri-

Creation Myth of the Mountain Pima

— · — · — · — · —

GOD MADE THE PEOPLE out of clay of the earth. These first people were not very good; so God changed many of these people into animals we see today. The lions, rabbits, coyotes, and other animals were all people before. Then God sent a great flood to destroy all the people because they were so bad. God made people again, this time smaller . . .

cahua Apache raided as far south from Arizona as Yécora and Maycoba during the 1880s. But the O'ob were ultimately successful in repulsing the Chiricahua incursions.

With the end of the Apache raids, the missionaries returned in force to Christianize the O'ob's homeland. In their wake, *blancos,* "Mexicans," staked much of the O'ob's fertile ground for cattle, lumber, mining, and now marijuana.

This tug-of-war over ancestral ground continues to this day.

Some say that the new highway brought the latest migration of settlers into the heartland of the O'ob. Like the trans-sierra Chihuahua al Pacífico railroad that brought change upon the Tarahumara a hundred miles south, Highway 16 is the last highway to breach the 750-mile-long Sierra Madre Occidental. It is a stomach-wrenching engineering marvel of relentless switchbacks that links Hermosillo, Sonora, with Chihuahua, Chihuahua. But with this narrow ribbon of asphalt, the twenty-first century has come hurtling toward one of the Southwest's least-known indigenous groups. And the O'ob now fear the Mestizo and Mexican strangers, more than the cries of the *onza* or the furtive band of Chiricahua Apache who have long been rumored still to dwell in the sierra. But if Geronimo's children are still living in the impenetrable barrancas of the northern Sierra Madre, they are not leaving the

A boy plays hide-and-seek while his sister collects paja, "pine needles," which are used in making adobe bricks. (Sonora, Mexico)

nineteenth century to face modern life in frontier-style Sonora.

Today, an estimated 2,000 O'ob still live in the Sierra Madre heartland. But some of the O'ob have retreated deeper into the sierra to live in caves or small rancherías, as they have for no one knows how long. Others travel seasonally to the rich farmland of Ciudad Obregón to work as migrant laborers when work cannot be had in the mountain sawmills. But others, especially those living in the historic communities of Yécora, Maycoba, and Yepachic, are still holding their ground after all these years.

One such O'ob is Cruzita Lao Rodríguez, and she can still be seen stalking the wooded sierra, plucking fragile herbs from the stony ground with her gnarled hands. She doesn't remember how old she is, but this she has lived: she is a *curendera,* medicine woman, and the people she continues to cure in her twilight hours are the O'ob; they are distant cousins to Arizona's Pima, and Cruzita is living proof that the O'ob will not let their culture slip easily from their grasp.

Born in Maycoba, eighty-year-old Cristóbal Galaviz López is a sobador, *"traditional healer," to the O'ob. (Sonora, Mexico)*

So is the humble Padre David José Beaumont. Here, where the first padres once rode mules into the Sierra Madre in hopes of extinguishing a Native culture in order to "save" it, you will now see a bearded American priest racing a blue, stake-side truck against the tide of time trying to preserve one.

In the quiet hills beyond Cruzita's pinewood dwelling, the padre has built a healing center so O'ob elders can continue to practice traditional medicine. Ovens for making bread have also been built under his direction, the base of what he hopes one day will evolve into O'ob-owned and operated businesses. He is encouraging the resurgence in traditional O'ob arts so their work can be displayed in a modest cultural museum he also plans to build. And, with O'ob translator Bertha Alicia Aguilar-Valenzuela, he has begun recording the ancient O'ob creation stories. But what is most important to the O'ob's cultural survival, perhaps, is the padre's restoration of the crumbling adobe walls of the church of San Francisco Javier de Maycoba; established in 1676 by Jesuit missionary Pedro Matías Goní, it has long since served as the sacred center for the O'ob's traditional ceremonies such as *Semana Santa*, "Easter week," where Christian beliefs mix with indigenous practices.

A bearded Pedro Lao Negrete is once more born of clay during Semana Santa. *(Sonora, Mexico)*

It is here, within this ceremonial ground, that the O'ob are once more born of clay. It was here, under Father sun and Mother moon, that the O'ob adopted me into their ancient ritual.

The road for me to reach this point was long but serendipitous.

It was December, and I was racing across the Sierra Madre, en route to photographing a story on the tragic plight of Tarahumara babies, when I saw what looked like a monk in brown robes carrying a small tree along the highway. I stopped the truck, because nothing had ever looked more incongruous to me in the Sierra Madre than the apparition this strange *güero,* "white man," projected in the afternoon sunlight. I was better prepared to see an *onza.* He had a shaggy beard; a long strand of black beads and a cross dangled from his waist; and on his feet were flimsy brown sandals.

Was it the padre to the Pimas? I wondered.

Years earlier I'd clipped an article from a Mexican newspaper about a padre who lived with the Pimas near the Tarahumara. I put it in my files in hopes of one day finding him. I wanted to see if these Pima had adapted any differently to the Sierra Madre than had the neighboring Tarahumara, and I wanted to know if they still had any contact with their desert-dwelling cousins in Arizona.

I ran back up the highway and looked at the tall man in brown robes. "Padre David?" I said.

"Yes," he answered. A Pima boy was lugging the old axe they had used to cut down the Christmas tree.

"I've been looking for you for two years," I said.

From that moment on, I realized, I had finally crossed the path that would lead me to the O'ob.

Four months later, O'ob elder Juan Rodríguez was using a sharp stick to paint my face with sacred white clay. Like the other O'ob participating in the four-day-and-night-long ceremony, my eyebrows and upper lip were also painted with black charcoal and my head was covered with a red bandana. By little more than asking Juan what the wet clay felt like on his face once it dried, I found myself suddenly adopted into their ancient ritual as a *fariseo,* or pharisee. And wherever they went throughout the long, sunny days and the cold, sleepless nights, I eagerly followed. I joined them for the holy adoration of San Francisco. I joined them in their government-sanctioned highway roadblocks, where they had collected *cuotas,* or tolls, to help pay for the ceremony. I joined them as they climbed the steep hillsides of Maycoba and went from house to house to fill their metal cups with fermented corn beer called *hún váki.* And I joined them when they snuffed out the fires of those who had failed to douse them for Easter Sunday.

Yet, from the beginning, their openness was moving; it reminded me of the Apache. I felt honored that the O'ob had shared such an important part of their culture with me, but at the time all I could think to say to them was, "In two days, you've offered your friendship to me the way no one in my own culture would do." The O'ob, in turn, told me it was *their* honor because I had traveled so far to meet them. But I didn't know just how much of an honor it was for the O'ob until Holy Friday, the day before the ritual wrestling match between the *fariseos* and *blancos.* This part of their Easter ceremony symbolized the current struggle between Mexicans and Mestizos over the O'ob's ancestral land. Everyone present had gathered into two large groups, and, as a prelude to the next day, each side playfully taunted the other. Suddenly, three masked *blancos* lassoed my hands and dragged me into a three-on-one, dirt-eating wrestling match. Then the O'ob jumped into the melee and, without raising a hand to stop it, they cried out in Spanish, "No! You cannot touch him. He is one of us. He is a *fariseo!*" A hush went over the crowd.

We got up, shook hands, wiped the blood off our noses and faces, and laughed off the nervous surge of adrenalin. Then the O'ob *capitán* turned to me and said, "They cannot touch you. You are one of us. You are a *fariseo.*"

Rosa Galaviz cares for her infant daughter in
their pinewood dwelling in the Sierra Madre.
(Sonora, Mexico)

Padre David José Beaumont catches a nap in the
Sierra Madre during his work among the O'ob.
(Sonora, Mexico)

Padre David José Beaumont among O'ob children.

(Sonora, Mexico)

Curandera, *"medicine woman,"* Cruzita Lao
Rodriguez weaves a palm-fiber basket in
her house. (Sonora, Mexico)

José de Jesús Miramón teaches O'ob children in
their one-room schoolhouse in the Sierra Madre.
(Sonora, Mexico)

*The difference between two cultures is illustrated
by the white-faced O'ob drummer and the
Mexican musicians. (Sonora, Mexico)*

Fariseo capitán *Juan Ramón Rodríguez Galaviz*
has a moment of reflection before Semana
Santa *ceremony begins. (Sonora, Mexico)*

O'ob fariseos *dance among masked* blancos,
"Mexicans," who portray Judios, *"Judas" figures*
during Semana Santa. *(Sonora, Mexico)*

Elder fariseos *at the ancient church of Sonora's*
San Francisco Javier de Maycoba.

PEOPLE OF THE *Desert*

Pápago / *Tohono O'odham*

Evening is falling,
At evening I run.
Far, far, to Baboquivari
I run and run...

PATRICIO LÓPEZ, SHAMAN AND EAGLE KILLER

FROM THE 7,734-FOOT SUMMIT of Baboquivari Peak, the vast ancestral lands of the O'odham run to the horizon in every direction: To the east, the Santa Catalina, the Rincón, and the Santa Rita mountains form the majestic eastern limits; to the north, the undulating course of the Gila River forms the lush northern boundary; to the west, the endless sweep of Sonoran desert forms the western horizon; and to the southwest, the drifting sand seas and deep volcanic craters of El Gran Desierto form the southwestern borderlands.

Long the landmark for early Spanish explorers, Baboquivari Peak is still considered sacred to the O'odham; it is the dwelling place of I'itoi, and he is the father of their creation. How I'itoi created the O'odham, however, is not a simple story for any layperson to tell. Once compared to the Book of Genesis, the complete version of the O'odham's creation story took four nights during the winter soltice, "when the sun stands still," to weave the dreaming with the singing for all those who had gathered to listen. One beginning, recorded by Juan Dolores, goes like this:

"Long ago, they say, when the earth was not yet finished, darkness lay upon the water, and they rubbed each other. The sound they made was like the sound at edges of a pond. There, on the water, in the darkness, in the noise, and in a very strong wind, a child was born."

The child was called *I'itoi,* or "Elder Brother." Together with Earthmaker and Coyote, he prepared the world for the Tohono O'odham, "People of the Desert."

Ethnographers and archaeologists have their own theories as to how the O'odham came to be. One hypothesis suggests a tenuous connection between the Tohono O'odham (formerly called the Pápago) and the Akimel O'odham (once

LEFT TO RIGHT: *Wade Escalante, Zack Ortega, Sheldon Escalante, Elvina Valisto, and Denise Martinez gather at a traditional saguaro camp to collect cactus fruit. (Arizona)*

known as the Pima) with the Hohokam, who disappeared from central Arizona about A.D. 1400. The most plausible explanation for this conjecture is that the Aztec plague was carried north from Mesoamerica centuries before the arrival of the Spaniards and the ensuing wave of epidemics caused the demise of the Hohokam. But there still remains a gap of 170 years between the Hohokam's collapse and the arrival of the O'odham that cannot be traced back through either their oral histories or calendar-stick memories. And what puzzles scientists most is that, in spite of this blank page during what they call the Dark Ages of the Southwest, the Tohono O'odham and Akimel O'odham had adapted to the Sonoran desert in ways remarkably similar to the Hohokam.

The Spaniards called the limitless desert lands of the O'odham *papaguería,* and not long after their arrival in 1540, they recognized that the O'odham had ingenious ways for adapting to its harsh environs. The Akimel O'odham, or Pima, lived and farmed peaceably along the course of Gila River; the confluence of the Gila, Salt, and Verde rivers created some of the richest agricultural land in the Sonoran desert. The Tohono O'odham, or Pápago, traveled seasonally across less-productive desert lands between summer field villages, where they practiced floodwater agriculture, and winter villages, where they settled near mountain springs and tended to small fields. The Hia Ced O'odham, or Sand Pápago, however, were cursed with the most bleak and desolate reaches of *papaguería.*

Bordered in the east by the Sierra del Ajo, on the north by the Gila River, on the west by the lower Colorado River, and on the south by the Gulf of California, this 8,000-square-mile Empty Quarter was the ancestral land of the Hia Ced O'odham, "People of the Sand." It is a hard country that rarely offered them more than a torturous struggle with merciless elements. Summertime temperatures soar beyond 120 degrees; rain, when it slakes this parched ground, seldom amounts to more than four inches a year. And sources of living water like *Aĩwaipa,* "small springs," and *Váketa,* "reeds," could usually be counted on one hand. Never believed to have numbered much more than 500 people, the Hia Ced O'odham alone knew how to sustain life in this austere desert.

More recently, however, Julian Hayden, a respected archaeologist, has proposed that there may have been two distinct groups of Hia Ced O'odham: The Pinacateños roamed the black lava desert and lunarscape of *Scuk Do'ag,* "black mountain," more commonly known as the Sierra del Pinacate in the

Creation Myth of the Pápago

— · — · — · — · —

LONG AGO, WHEN THE EARTH was not yet finished, darkness lay upon the water, and they rubbed each other. The sound they made was like the sound at edges of a pond. There, on the water, in the darkness, in the noise, and in a very strong wind, a child was born.

frontier of Sonora; while the Areneños searched the sere desert valleys that pushed up the exposed fangs of two dozen basin-and-range-type mountains in what became Arizona.

Tinajas, or "rock tank" rain catchments, with names like *Otoxakam* ("where there is bulrush"), *Tjukomókamt júupo* ("black head pools"), and *Óovak* ("where the arrows were shot"), linked the seasonal encampments of the Hia Ced O'odham, which stretched to the far ends of their immense domain. And when the "Sand Pápago" wandered beyond the marginal haven of these precious *tinajas*—which they often did during ritual journeys to the Gulf to sing the sacred songs and gather salt, shells, and fish—they survived on the acidic moisture of the *hía tadk,* "sand root," a parisitic, potato-like tuber that still grows in the billowing dunes of El Gran Desierto.

Only the Jesuit missionary, explorer, and cartographer Padre Eusebio Francisco Kino had the skill and stamina to repeatedly match wits with the Pinacateños' and Areneños' private infernos. But the route Padre Kino is often credited with pioneering actually followed the tracks of the Hia Ced O'odham from Aîwaipa (Quitobaquito Springs) west to A'oot (Dome, near Yuma). It was near the end of this ancient path at Óovak, or Tinajas Altas, that Kino observed a group of Hia Ced O'odham in 1699: "Here Manje counted thirty naked and poverty-stricken Indians who lived on roots, lizards, and other wild foods." It was one of the first eyewitness accounts of the desperate life the Hia Ced O'odham endured in the northern reaches of what the Spaniards called Pimería Alta, "Land of the Upper Pima Indians."

This historic sighting also foreshadowed the horror of death by dehydration that haunted American settlers and Mexican miners who tried to follow the tracks of Padre Kino and the Hia Ced O'odham from one distant *tinaja* to the next a century and a half later. Whatever the route may have been called in the Hia Ced O'odham's tongue—and others like the Hohokam shell trail that stretched south from Gila Bend to the Gulf—non-Natives lucky enough to survive the journey swore it was the Camino del Diablo, "the Road of the Devil." For good reason, during the 1850s alone an estimated 400 people died of thirst along this notorious desert track, for want of the savviness of the Hia Ced O'odham—or Padre Kino.

Perilous trails like the Camino del Diablo, as well as the more heavily traveled Gila Trail immediately to the north, did not bode well for the future of the O'odham people. These trails carried a relentless tide of horses, wagons, miners, settlers, and soldiers across the heart of the O'odham's ancestral land, and with this tremendous western migration to California came the political pressure for the United States to buy 30,000 square miles of northwest Mexico for $10 million.

When the Gadsden Purchase was finalized on December 30, 1853, the an-cestral lands of the Tohono O'odham were effectively divided between Sonora and Arizona. And lands that had already been heavily missionized by Jesuits during the early 1700s came under even greater pressure from Spanish miners and cattlemen south of the border, and from Anglo settlers, missionaries, and "Apaches" to the north. The O'odham world

Eighty-year-old cowboy Ed Kisto runs a cattle ranch at the foot of the Baboquivari Mountains. (Arizona)

dwindled before their eyes, and by 1916 they had become a people divided among reservations at Sells, San Xavier, Gila Bend, and Ajo.

But even in the best of times, the Tohono O'odham's parched desert tracts never offered them much more than a meager living. Their territory did not have the vast coal reserves of the Navajo, or the dense stands of commercial timber and lush grazing lands of the Western Apache, or even the rich agricultural lands of the neighboring Pima. Gaining a toehold in the Anglo economy was difficult, since the best commercial prospect for their land was cattle ranching. A tough proposition anywhere, cattle ranching was even more dubious an endeavor for the Tohono O'odham because their average cow-calf operation required 350 acres of Sonoran desert per head per year—and there was scant drinking water for the ranchers or their livestock. Today, however, the Tohono O'odham economy has received a boost from casino gambling, but this is a divisive issue for Native Americans throughout the Southwest, an economic bounty that some see as inimical to the heart of traditional spiritual beliefs.

Stella Tucker carries on the O'odham tradition of collecting saguaro fruit in the Tucson Mountains each June. (Arizona)

Compared to the reservation lands of the Akimel O'odham, the lands of the Tohono O'odham today are still seemingly endless; home to an estimated seven thousand people, the reservation occupies 2,855,430 square acres in southwestern Arizona. And in lands as vast as these my travels led me in many directions over a long period of time: In the midst of the worst drought to curse the region in years, I visited 70-year-old rancher Ed Kisto at Chiuli Shaik; following the tradition of early Tohono O'odham stockmen, who tended the seed herds of cattle first introduced by Padre Kino, Kisto runs a successful cow-calf operation in the Sonoran desert scrub that fans out from the base of Baboquivari Peak.

During the waning days of spring, I visited administrator Verna Morrow at San Simón High School near the western edge of the reservation; with her preteen students she has successfully revived the ancient stickball game of *toka,* and today they travel throughout the region playing exhibition games for other Native Americans in hopes that they, too, will revive their own athletic traditions. On the eve of Arizona's "summer monsoon," I visited Stella Tucker at her saguaro camp in the Tucson Mountains; here, in one of the most verdant stands of saguaro in the region, she teaches young men and women the long tradition of their people by collecting saguaro fruit for making preserves.

During the summer soltice, I visited Quito Wa:k in northern Sonora for the annual harvest ceremony called *wi:kida;* long considered "lost" by outsiders, Arizona O'odham still join their kin south of the border to celebrate this ancient rite of renewal. And during one of the hottest summer days on record, I ventured into the burnt blast of desert the Sand Pápago have always called home to visit with Chico Shuni; this brave elder still maintains a lone vigil of the Hia Ced O'odham's land that dates back deep into the time of legend. Few days in my life were more inspirational: here was the living embodiment of a people who wrested a living and a culture where few others could survive.

Chico Shuni maintains his lone vigil over the Hia Ced
O'odham's ancestral land. The vigil has been kept by
his predecessors for thousands of years. (Arizona)

The Hia Ced O'odham, "People of the Sand," take
their name from the austere desert lands they
inhabited in Arizona.

*In 1697, San Cayetano Tumacacori was established
by missionary Padre Kino as a* visita *among
the Pápago. (Arizona)*

Tohono O'odham elders dance to traditional
waila music at the Fiesta de San Francisco in
Tumacacori National Monument. (Arizona)

Tribal leader Eugenio Velasco Ortega and his wife

Herlinda León Pacheco at home in Quito Wa:k.

(Sonora, Mexico)

The ancient O'odham stickball game of toka *has been revived by Verna Morrow at San Simón High School. (Arizona)*

Raymundo Montejo Robles at home in Quito
Wa:k. Mexican O'odham like Raymundo still call
themselves Pápago.

OPPOSITE: *Rafael Garcia of Quito Wa:k, Sonora, is
a* pascola *dancer.*

PEOPLE OF THE
Rivers

Pima / *Akimel O'odham*
Mojave / *Makháv*
Hualapai / *Hwalapay*

From under Wikame, the sacred
mountain,
Tu'djupa, the younger god, took a piece
of river cane and broke it into pieces.
He called each piece the name
of a tribe:
Hualapai, Havasupai, Hopi, and Paiute.
He carried them to the East and laid
them down and they came to life.

Hualapai Creation Myth

*I*T IS DIFFICULT TO STAND atop any mountain and see the ancestral lands of Arizona's riverine cultures, simply because the geography is so vast and diverse. But climb to the 7,657-foot summit of *Wikedjasa,* "Chopped-up Mountains," the sacred mountain of the Kewevkapaya Yavapai, and from its craggy Four Peaks you can trace the beginnings of wild rivers that formed those distant cultures.

To the south, the Salt River winds out of the dark serpentine abyss of Salt River Canyon and joins the Verde and Gila rivers in the heart of the Sonoran desert. The Pima took their name from these pulsating rivers, and called themselves Akimel O'odham, "People of the River." Occupying the abandoned lands of the Hohokam, the Pima depended on a digging-stick economy centered on *ak chin* farming, whereby floodwater was funneled into the fields of maíz and wheat they ingeniously cultivated in their sparse desert lands.

From the confluence of the Salt and Verde rivers, the Gila River wanders southwest across the blistering Arizona desert 200 miles to the lower Colorado River. Along this lush fluvial corridor, the Maricopa farmed and hunted and gathered much like the neighboring Pima. But the *pi:pa's,* "the People," as the Maricopa call themselves, also made use of an ancient trail system along the Gila River for weeklong trading forays that enabled them to barter with the distant Cocopa for *u v sax,* the Pai-pai's "rotten tobacco."

If you travel upstream from the confluence of the Gila and Colorado rivers, north toward the mountain once called Wikame, you will enter the scorching desert badlands of the Mojave. Known as the *makhá v,* "people who live along the river," the Mojave also traveled extensively to trade; but unlike the Maricopa they crossed the sere Mojave Desert to the

with distant coastal tribes, often running a hun-
...lay.

...northeast from the lower Colorado River along
...rade route that linked the Pacific Coast to the
...in New Mexico and you will enter the impos-
...nd canyon country of the Hualapai; known as
"Ponderosa Pine People,"
...inhabited lands from the
...ver in the western Grand
...h all the way to the Bill
...er; they were renowned
...at hunting the Canyon's
...orn sheep for meat and
...they traded with distant
...z, squash, and other food

...e borders formed by the
...Colorado, Gila, and Verde
...,000-square-mile tract of
...na that was home to the
...n as the *paca*, "the People,"
the Yavapai lived like no other desert-
dwelling people in Arizona simply
because they adapted to environmental extremes that ranged from cool
pine forests to burning creosote flats.
Principally hunters and gatherers, the
men wore deerhead masks to hunt

*Sunlight and storm enshroud a climber on the
summit of 7,645-foot Four Peaks. The sacred
mountain of the Kewevkapaya Yavapai, it is
known to them as Wikedjasa, "Chopped-up
Mountains." (Arizona)*

their prey with bows and arrows in the higher elevations,
while the women gathered food such as *mescal* (the heart of
the century plant) in the lower elevations.

Ethnographers link the Pima to the Papago, and the Mojave, Hualapai, and Yavapai to the ancient Yuman peoples, but the creation myths of the river people are as distinct as the lands they inhabited. Fortunately, some of these origin stories have been recorded and translated by native peoples.

One of the original versions of the Pima creation story was told by *Comalk-Hawk-Kih,* "Thin Buckskin." The Pima elder was one of the last of the *see-nee-yaw-kum,* "traditional storytellers," and through his nephew Edward Hubert Wood, he told the story to writer William Lloyd. The time was 1903: It was a hot September night, coyotes were howling in the distance, and a full moon had risen over the desert peaks when he weaved the story of his people's birth; it starts like this:

"In the beginning there was no earth, no water—nothing. There was only a person, *Juh-wert-a-Mah-kai,* 'Doctor of the Earth.'

"He just floated, for there was no place for him to stand upon. There was no sun, no light, and he just floated about in the darkness, which was Darkness itself.

"He wandered around in the no-where till he thought he had wandered enough. Then he rubbed on his breast and rubbed out *moah-haht-tack,* that is, perspiration, or greasy earth. This he rubbed out on the palm of his hand and held out. It tipped over three times, but the fourth time it staid [sic] straight in the middle of the air and there it remains now as the world."

The Mojave were born after the spirit Mastamhó killed Sky Rattlesnake, and today they still find their spiritual strength in the sacred stones and pinnacles of *Hum-Me-Chump* along the lower Colorado River. The Hualapai were born

Creation Myth of the Pima

— · — · — · — · — · — · —

*I*N THE BEGINNING, there was no earth, no water—nothing. There was only a person, *Juh-wert-a-Mah-kai*, Doctor of the earth. He just floated, for there was no place for him to stand upon. There was no sun, no light, and he just floated about in the darkness . . .

from Spirit Mountain, once called Wikame, by the hand of Tu'djupa, and they still gain their spiritual strength from the sacred springs at *Mata:widita* in the depths of the Grand Canyon. The Yavapai were born beneath a bottomless well and emerged from the earth at *Ahagaskiaywa,* "Montezuma's Well," and today they find their spiritual strength in the holy waters near the foot of the redrocks they call *wipuk.*

Living, as they did, near the Southwest's principal water sources, the Pima, Mojave, and Hualapai—among others—discovered they also lived along principal travel corridors used by explorers, trappers, and settlers who would ultimately change the course of their destinies.

Foremost among these outsiders, perhaps, was Padre Eusebio Francisco Kino; the Jesuit missionary visited the Pima as early as 1691, driving seed herds of cattle and horses that would change the character of the people and the face of the Southwest. Between 1697 and 1701, the tireless Padre Kino rode a staggering 7,500 miles of "unexplored trails" throughout much of the harshest reaches of Pimería Alta and, in spite of the Pima's revolts against the Spaniards, he helped establish two dozen missions and *visitas.* It was Padre Kino's travels along the ancient routes of the Maricopa and Sand Pápago, however, that later foreshadowed the difficult jour-

America's first cowboys, Native Americans punched cattle for Spanish missionaries as early as 1770. Today, their great equestrian tradition lives on in rodeo. Yavapai Arleigh Banaha gained national acclaim-and broken bones-as a top rodeo bullfighter and clown. (Prescott, Arizona)

neys of immigrants who followed the Gila Trail and Camino del Diablo during the 1850s.

A century and a half before Padre Kino's death in 1711, Spanish explorer Melchior Díaz had already visited the Mojave along the Colorado River; Díaz was the first to describe the Mojave's connection to the river and why the Spaniards named it the *Río Tizón*, "firebrand river." In *Obregón's History of Sixteenth-Century Explorations in Western American*, Díaz was quoted: "The natives cross it, in spite of its width, on great rafts of agave. On this day they cross paddling with their feet and carrying a lighted torch in their hands in order to keep fire on both sides."

But it wasn't until Spanish missionary Francisco Tomás Garcés traversed the Mojave Desert in February 1776 that a non-Indian described the long-distance prowess of the ancient Mojave runners and traders. Garcés, writing from somewhere in the forlorn interior of the Mojave Desert, reported: "Here I met four Indians who had come from Santa Clara to traffic in shell beads. They were carrying no food supply, nor even bows for hunting. Noticing my astonishment at this, where there is nothing to eat, they said, 'We Jamajabs can withstand hunger and thirst for as long as four days,' giving me to understand they were hardy men." Like the lower Colorado River corridor, the Mojave Trail was used by settlers, but they traveled it in droves to reach Nuestra de Señora de los Angeles.

During his epic 2,000-mile roundabout journey from Tucson's Mission San Xavier del Bac to California's Mission San Gabriel, Padre Garcés also visited the Hualapai in northwestern Arizona. But it wasn't until Lieutenant Joseph Christmas Ives' 1858 river survey probed Hualapai country from the west, and Major John Wesley Powell's 1869 river expedition explored it from the east, that the Hualapai also began to feel the crush of outsiders following the 35th parallel across their ancestral lands to reach California.

In the winter of 1875 the Yavapai to the south fared even worse; 1,500 Verde River Yavapai were forcibly relocated by soldiers and marched at gunpoint 180 miles to the San Carlos Apache Indian Reservation. It was a torturous journey that killed 115 Yavapai, and it coursed through the same rugged country where, three years earlier, 76 Kewevkapaya Yavapai were massacred by soldiers at Skeleton Cave.

River peoples who survived the forced marches and slaughters had to endure grim reservation life. They were often banished to distant lands and thrown in with tribes culturally distinct from their own. In 1859 the River Yuman–speaking Maricopa were put together with the Southern Uto-Aztecan–speaking Pima on the Gila River Indian Reservation; the Upland Yuman–speaking Yavapai were lumped together with the Apachean-speaking Apache on the Verde River at Fort McDowell. And on the lower Colorado River, the remaining River Yuman–speaking Mojave who had not been relocated to distant Fort McDowell found their small reservation occupied by linguistic strangers as diverse as the Shoshonean-speaking Chemehuevi, the Uto-Aztecan–speaking Hopi, and Apachean-speaking Navajo.

Despite the degrading loss of ancestral lands, the spirit of the river people has persevered. Along the banks of the Colorado River, I visited with Mojave elder Donna Stanley, who has revived the Mojave's ancient Bird Dance; in a spiritual world formed by dreams and visions, the Mojave Bird Dance has instilled pride in the women of the tribe as well as the people who come to witness it. In distant Chandler, I visited with Pima elders Gwendolyn Paul and Barnaby Lewis, who have revived the Basket Dance among the young; renowned for their weave and design, Pima baskets were traditionally used for winnowing mesquite beans, carrying the harvests of maíz and wheat, and storing the sacred relics of ancestors. In Casa Grande, Window Rock, and elsewhere throughout Arizona and the West, I photographed Native Americans carrying on their own cowboy traditions in modern rodeo arenas. Odd as it may seem to those raised on Saturday afternoon shoot-em-ups, the native peoples were America's first cowboys: They were punching cattle for Spanish missionaries as early as 1770, a century before the first non-Indian cowboys donned batwing chaps and Sugarloaf sombreros to drive herds of Texas longhorns along the Chisholm Trail to the railhead at Kansas City.

Akimel O'odham elder Barnaby Lewis sings trational songs for the Basket dance. (Chandler, Arizona)

Near the end of my long journey to meet Arizona's river people, I was ultimately drawn back to the river itself. Because it is here, in the western Grand Canyon, that the Hualapai had known the Colorado River centuries before Major John Wesley Powell first explored it. It is here that Hualapai boatmen like Roderick Matuck and Havasupai boatmen like Dennie Wescogame still ply the sacred waters from which Tu'djupa first made the people out of cane. And it is here in the mesmerizing embrace of this great river that all people still come to life.

*Arizona's Superstition Mountain stands 5,057 feet
high and is at the center of the Akimel O'odham
creation story. They know it as Kakatak Tamai,
"Crooked Top Mountain." (Arizona)*

*Hohokam petroglyphs mark the southern limits
of the Akimel O'odham's ancestral range in the
Picacho Mountains. (Arizona)*

*The boots of a Native American bull rider are
lashed on to keep them from flying off during
the ride. (Tucson, Arizona)*

An Akimel O'odham flies high at the O'odham
Tash Days rodeo. (Casa Grande, Arizona)

Traditional Bird singers and dancers include
members of the Maricopa, Quechan, Cocopa, and
Akimel O'odham. (Chandler, Arizona)

Mojave Bird dancer. (Parker, Arizona)

Havasupai boatman Dennie Wescogame guides
tourists through ancestral lands in the western
Grand Canyon. (Arizona)

Hualapai boatman Roderick "Archie" Matuck
stands near the sacred waters of Mata:widita in
the western Grand Canyon. (Arizona)

PEOPLE OF THE *Mesas*

Navajo / *Diné*

In beauty I walk
With beauty before me I walk
With beauty behind me I walk
With beauty above me I walk
With beauty above and
about me I walk
It is finished in beauty
It is finished in beauty.

FROM "THE NIGHT CHANT" OF THE NAVAJO

T<small>HROUGH THE GOLDEN EYE</small> of Window Rock in northern Arizona, you can envision the four geographical monuments that mark the physical limits of the Navajo Reservation: the Grand Canyon to the west; Glen Canyon and Rainbow Bridge to the north; the southern Rocky Mountains to the east; and the Mogollon Rim to the south. The Navajo have revered these landforms since their creation, and the names they have given them reveal their mythic dimension. The Grand Canyon is *'Ashiih,* the cave that is home to Salt Woman. The spectacular arch of Rainbow Bridge is *Nonnezoshi,* "Rainbow Rock-span," where the Cloud and Rain People were born. The lofty, snow-capped peaks of the southern Rockies hold *Sísnaadjínii,* "Horizontal Black Belt," where sacred ceremonies are still performed. And the forested lakes and summer retreat of the Mogollon Rim are *Dzil Bii'dzooldzisii,* the "Mountain with Pockets."

Now look through the window called *Tseghahodzani,* "Perforated Rock," and you will see the four sacred mountains that embody the legends and define the four directions of the Navajo's spiritual universe. In ceremonial order, there is *Sísnaajínii,* the sacred mountain of the east; it was fastened to the earth by lightning and is also known as the 14,317-foot Blanca Peak of Colorado's Sangre de Cristo Mountains. There is *Dzil Dotllizii,* "Turquoise Mountain," the sacred mountain of the south; it was fastened to the earth by a great flint knife and is also known as the 11,389-foot Mount Taylor of New Mexico's San Mateo Mountains. There is *Dook'o'oosliid,* "Never Thaws on Top," the sacred mountain of the west; it was fastened to the earth by a sunbeam and is also known as the 12,633-foot San Francisco Peaks of northern Arizona. And there is *Dibé Ntssa,* "Big Mountain Sheep," the sacred mountain of the north; it was fastened to the earth by a rainbow and is also known as the 13,225-foot Hesperus Peak of Colorado's La Plata range. Medicine men and traditionalists still make pilgrimages to each of these sacred mountains to collect soil for their *dzileezh bijish,* "medicine pouches," for use in their prayers and ceremonies.

Born to the Red-streak-into-water clan, medicine man Floyd Laughter explained the importance of these sacred mountains to ethnographer Karl Luckert in 1976: "Each of these mountains has a story, prayer, song, and ceremony associated with it. And all are interconnected, including the sacred songs. And within that sacred land we were born, and continue to be born. And within this sacred land we will reach old age. This was laid down and decreed to us from the beginning."

Born to both the Many Goats and Coyote Pass People clans, Miss Navajo contestant Candice John of Page, Arizona, demonstrates corn grinding for the Traditional Skills competition.

Within the four corners of the Diné's universe marked by these sacred mountains is *dinétah,* "the land." It is a 25,000-square-mile tract of the 6,000-foot-high Colorado Plateau, and it covers the Four Corners region of New Mexico, Arizona, Utah, and Colorado. This is where the largest group of Native Americans—an estimated 220,000—live, work, and revere their land through ceremonial "sings," or chantways. Scattered throughout Dinetah are other awesome landforms made by the hands of their gods and the Holy Ones: the redrock monoliths of Monument Valley, the black volcanic peaks of Agathla and Shiprock, the green pine belts of the Chuska and Lukachukai Mountains, the kaleido-

scopic sweep of Black Mesa and the Painted Desert, and the
deep canyons of the Little Colorado River Gorge and
Canyon de Chelly; they, too, all have legends. So do hundreds
of other sacred mountains, mesas, buttes, rocks, lakes, and
streams—and others known only to the medicine men who
still perform the sacred ceremonies that hold together the
very fabric of their spiritual world.

The story of the Diné's origin, the one most often told,
is familiar. About 50,000 B.C., hunters and gatherers called
Southern Athapaskans crossed the Siberian land bridge and
migrated south through the millennia down the length of
the Rocky Mountains; between A.D. 1200 and 1500
they dispersed throughout the region that one day
would be called Four Corners. These people called themselves Diné, "the People." It was only much later that
others would call them Navajo.

The Diné's own version of their origin is very different. Over five hundred songs, sung in ceremonial suc-
cession over many days and nights, tell the story of
their creation. So the story can only be told by a medicine man. One such "singer" was Hasteen Klah. In
Navajo Creation Myth: The Story of Emergence, Mary C. Wheelwright recorded the medicine men's myths and great ceremonies that tell the full story of the Diné's creation. A verse
from *N'dloe,* the Hail Chant, called "The Song of Creating
People," was sung by Hasteen Klah; it goes like this:

> The sky, its life am I, hozhoni, hozhoni
> The mountains, their life am I, hozhoni, hozhoni
> Rain-mountain, its life am I, hozhoni, hozhoni
> Changing-Woman, her life am I, hozhoni, hozhoni
> The Sun, its life am I, hozhoni, hozhoni
> Talking God, his life am I, hozhoni, hozhoni

Creation Myth of the Navajo

The sky, its life am I,
hozhoni, hozhoni
The mountains, their life am I,
hozhoni, hozhoni
Rain-mountain, its life am I,
hozhoni, hozhoni
Changing-Woman, her life am I,
hozhoni, hozhoni
The Sun, its life am I,
hozhoni, hozhoni
Talking God, his life am I,
hozhoni, hozhoni

House God, his life am I, hozhoni, hozhoni
White Corn, its life am I, hozhoni, hozhoni
Yellow Corn, its life am I, hozhoni, hozhoni
Corn-pollen, its life am I, hozhoni, hozhoni
The corn-beetle, its life am I, hozhoni, hozhoni
Hozhoni, hozhoni, hozhoni
Hozhoni, hozhoni, hozhoni

The concept of *hozhoni* has been variously interpreted to mean beauty and peace, and the Diné's harmonious relationship between the sky, the earth, and all the natural elements they continue to sustain.

The beauty and harmony in the Diné's universe started to unravel in 1630, when Padre Alonso de Benavides first noted the Diné living west of the Río Grande pueblos and east of the Hopi mesas. The Franciscan missionary distinguished the Diné from other Apachean-speaking peoples by calling them *Apaches de Nabajó,* for their skill at raising "large planted fields" of maize. At the time, the Diné were seminomadic hunter-gatherer agriculturalists; they collected juniper berries, piñon nuts, and yucca, hunted deer and rabbits, and raised staples such as corn, beans, and squash.

The introduction of the horse by Francisco Vásquez de Coronado in 1540, and later sheep and cattle by Spanish colonialists, changed forever the Diné's way of life. By 1855 an estimated 12,000 Diné were raising some 200,000 sheep and 10,000 horses and were producing 60,000 bushels of corn each season from 5,000 acres. A highly mobile mounted force, the Diné also reportedly raided the Río Grande pueblos to the east, as well as villages as far south as the Mexican states of Chihuahua and Durango. The Diné, in turn, were preyed upon by the Spaniards, who conquered New Mexico and kidnapped Diné children for their bustling slave trade. Until

1848 the Navajo were skilled warriors to be reckoned with; but that changed with the Treaty of Guadalupe Hidalgo, when their ancestral lands came under American sovereignty and they were pitted against overwhelming U.S. forces.

On August 31, 1849, the Diné's relationship with the United States reached a flash point: government troops murdered and scalped Diné leader Narbona and six of his men. The relentless thrust of New Mexican slave traders, and Mexican and American settlers vying over the Diné's land, drove the Diné to attack Fort Defiance in 1860; that battle prefaced the Long Walk, the most terrible chapter in the Diné's history.

Liana Lynn Cleveland of Fort Defiance, Arizona, dressed for the Traditional Song & Dance. (Window Rock, Arizona)

During General James H. Carleton and Kit Carson's devastating campaign throughout Navajoland, they captured 200 *cey'ni* Navajo in Canyon de Chelly; called *Tse zhini,* "Traprock," Canyon de Chelly was of great traditional importance to the Diné. Upon hearing of the *cey'ni*'s capture, some Diné traveled as far west as Havasupai in the western Grand Canyon; others escaped as far south as the Chiricahua Apache country; lead by Chief Hashkénniinii, others fled to southern Utah to hide behind the 10,416-foot Navajo Mountain. Here, they eluded the ruthless forces marshaled under mountain-man Kit Carson. They called their holy mountain *Naatsis'áán,* "Head of the Earth Woman," their Divine Shield of Protection. It was here that I had my formative experience among the Diné, Dinétah, and their spiritual beliefs.

Today, the Diné have a thriving economy compared to most Native Americans in the Southwest; it's based on coal leases, sheep and cattle ranching, lumber, tourism, and education. Yet their deep traditional beliefs led the Diné to vote out casino gambling. Their traditional life is vibrant, and each year the Diné invite everyone to Window Rock, Arizona, for their annual fair; here, visiting Diné and others can view the handiwork of their weaving and silversmithing, their traditional song and dance, their rodeo action, and their own Plains Indian powwow. They can also witness the young women vying for the title of Miss Navajo; she alone will travel the world to explain the Diné's modern and traditional ways.

My own journey among the Diné began many years ago, far to the west, when I lead a group of Tuba City High School students on a two-week "wilderness challenge" course around Navajo Mountain on the Utah-Arizona border. A week into our arduous trek, we veered off our route and went to look at Rainbow Bridge. Up to that point, I had felt a little awkward teaching Native Americans survival skills their forefathers might once have taught mine. When it came time to say the prayer of Protection to guarantee a safe journey after leaving Nonnezoshi, none of teens said it, although before we left Tuba City their elders had instructed them to offer the prayer.

We had no sooner passed beneath the Rainbow when a heavy wooden tripod fell out of the sky and crashed in the streambed a dozen feet in front of us. Bureau of Reclamation engineers were conducting a biannual survey to determine whether the encroaching waters of Lake Powell were undermining the soft sandstone formation of Rainbow Bridge and they had failed to anchor their tripod to the apex of Rainbow Bridge.

I thought about it, though only as a close call—one of the

"objective hazards" of visiting a crowded national monument ... until the next morning, when we went to take one last look at Nonnezoshi before continuing north around Navajo Mountain. Again we passed beneath the Rainbow without saying the prayer of Protection, and yet another wooden tripod fell out of the sky and exploded in the rocks in front of us.

When we returned to Tuba City a week later, elders explained that the events were the result of the prayer of Protection not having been said, and that no one was to pass beneath the Rainbow. Before Lake Powell was formed, they said, medicine men made frequent pilgrimages to the San Juan and Colorado rivers, and to Rainbow Bridge, to perform the sacred ceremonies.

A year later, I was leading a group of non-Indians up the 12,633-foot San Francisco Peaks when I saw a small snake slithering next to the U.S. Geological Survey benchmark. We were in subalpine tundra, a full 1,600 feet above the uppermost habitat of any North American snake, and it was cold enough to wear a down parka.

I was moved, not in a metaphysical sense. But why was I allowed to behold a snake on the very summit of Arizona where no snakes are supposed to be? And what about the tripods raining off the Rainbow a year earlier? Were they signs of some sort? That's when I first came to understand what the Diné have always believed, that their mountains are sacred and are still inhabited by their deities, in whatever form they take.

That is the beauty of the Diné's world: Within their sacred land, they were born. Within their sacred land, they continue to be born. Within their sacred land, they will reach old age.

So it was decreed in the beginning.

And it is still so.

Hozhoni, Hozhoni, Hozhoni.

Powwow Fancy dancer. (Window Rock, Arizona)

OPPOSITE: *Traditional weapons maker and
musician Aski-Ei-Bah "War Pony" Anderson.
(Window Rock, Arizona)*

Powwow Fancy Shawl dancer.

(Window Rock, Arizona)

Powwow Traditional dancer.
(Window Rock, Arizona)

Marvin Hardy (right) *and partner lead*
the Traditional Song & Dance.
(Window Rock, Arizona)

Women Shawl dancers. (Window Rock, Arizona)

Elsie Plummer of Yatahey, New Mexico, was born
of the Red-Streak-Running-into-Water and
Mexican clans.

World War II veteran James A. Kimble of
Montrose, Colorado, served with the 82nd and
101st Airborne Divisions.

Aisha Oldham of Window Rock, Arizona, wins first
place in the annual 4-H competition.

Marie H. Belone of Fort Defiance, Arizona, is dressed in turquoise and gold for the Traditional Song & Dance.

A GATHERING OF *Nations*

Long ago in the north
Lies the road of emergence.
Beyond our ancestors live,
Beyond we take our being.
Yet now we come southward,
For cloud flowers blossom here,
Here the lightning flashes,
Rain water here is falling.

From "The Turtle Dance Song" of the Tewa

ROM THE 11,301-FOOT SUMMIT of Mount Taylor in the San Mateo Mountains of northwestern New Mexico, you can gaze in the six directions of the Zuni world and see the enchanted mesas and the lush river valleys still inhabited by the Pueblo peoples. North is yellow and points to Sandy Lake, where the Tewa first entered the Pueblo world. East is white and points to the Great Plains, where the buffalo first entered the Pueblo world. South is red and points to Mexico, where the Spaniards first entered the Pueblo world. West is blue and points to the Pacific Ocean, where ancient trade goods entered the Pueblo world. The nadir is black and points to the underworld, from whence the Pueblo people first emerged into this world. The zenith is rainbow-hued and points to the sun, the first natural force to beam upon the Pueblo world.

Situated near the headwaters of the Zuni River on the west slope of the Continental Divide, Zuni was the largest of New Mexico's seventy-odd pueblos; at the time of Spanish contact, more than 5,000 people lived there. Still known as *halono wa,* "red ant place," Zuni was one of six principal villages—and four summer farming villages—the Zuni inhabited in homelands they call *siwin a,* a "Zuni place." Like the neighboring Navajo to the west, the Zuni were also hunter-gatherer-agriculturalists, but their farming techniques made use of small rectangular plots called *łatek inne,* "enclosed with sticks"; bordered by berms of adobe, these "waffle gardens" supported a variety of crops, such as chiles, melons, and herbs.

Perched atop 400-foot-high Ácoma Mesa on the east slope of the Continental Divide, 60 miles east of Zuni, the spectacular Keresan pueblo of Ácoma is the oldest Pueblo village; its settlement dates back to A.D. 900 and is thought to rival the Hopi pueblo of Old Oraibi as the oldest continuously inhabited settlement in the United States. Called *á ku* by the Keresan, Ácoma was once inhabited by 2,000 people and is situated at the foot of Mount Taylor overlooking Ácoma Creek; here the *á ku me ca,* as the Keresan from Ácoma call themselves, farmed, raised turkeys, and hunted deer.

The taking of deer was a sacred matter among Pueblo peoples, and the Keresan of Ácoma sought the council of a priest called Eagle Man to bless their hunting fetishes with song before a hunt. Beginning with the lion in the north, the verse was repeated four times, marking the east with the wildcat, the south with a lynx, and the west with a wolf:

> It comes alive
> It comes alive, alive, alive
> In the north mountain
> The lion comes alive
> In the north mountain, comes alive
> With this the prey animal
> Will have power to attract deer,
>   antelope;
> Will have power to be lucky.

Located at the confluence of the Río Chama and Río Grande 120 miles northeast of Ácoma, the twin river settlements of San Juan were the

Zuni Traditional dancer Alton Nastacio of Zuni, New Mexico.

northernmost of New Mexico's Tewa pueblos and were called both *ohke* and *yúngé,* "mockingbird place." The population was thought to number not more than 300 Tewas. Here the San Juan Tewa hunted deer, tilled corn, beans, and squash, and raised goats and sheep. They also revered their sacred mountain called *cikumu,* "obsidian covered." At this spiritual landmark to peace, no enemy blood was ever shed because, as San Juan Tewa scholar Alfonso Ortíz wrote: "It is the chief of all mountains, the most sacred thing we see each day."

The prehistory of the Pueblo peoples of San Juan, Ácoma, and Zuni has been difficult for ethnographers and archaeologists to trace with any certainty. Though the Pueblo peoples inhabited the vast ancestral lands of the *anaasází,* they don't like being linked to the *anaasází* because it is a Navajo term that means "enemy ancestors." While Pueblo peoples share many cultural traits and ceremonial practices, their languages are as distinct as their creation stories. When ceremonial items such as macaw feathers, red ochre, and abalone shells were being bartered throughout a vast network of trade routes, the Pueblo people often made use of sign language or a third mutually intelligible language because Zuni-speaking Zuni could not converse in their native tongue with the Keresan at Ácoma, any more than the Keresan speakers could understand the Northern Tewa–speaking people at San Juan.

So, too, the creation story of each of the Pueblo peoples differs from the others.

The sacred story of the Ácoma people begins like this: "They came out of the earth, from *Iatik',* the mother. They came out through a hole in the earth called *Shipap.* They crawled out like grasshoppers; their bodies were naked and soft. It was all dark; the sun had not yet risen. All the little people had their eyes closed; they hadn't opened them yet. *Iatik'* lined them all up in a row, facing

Creation Myth of the Acoma

— · — · — · — · —

*T*HEY CAME OUT OF THE EARTH, from *Iatik'*, the mother. They came out through a hole in the earth called *Shipap*. They crawled out like grasshoppers; their bodies were naked and soft. It was all dark; the sun had not yet risen. All the little people had their eyes closed. . .

east. Then she had the sun come. When it came up and shone on the babies' eyes, they opened."

The creation story of the San Juan Tewa also begins in the underworld, but at another sacred place, *Ohange pokwinge,* "Sand Lake." It was here that the Tewa's Summer Mother, *Kutsa-bukwi payokaga,* "Corn White," and their Winter Mother, *Kutsabukwi oyikaga,* "Ice Mother," were born. One Mother became the Father-Mother, and from them the people emerged. According to sacred Tewa beliefs, these first people went forth and populated the ten original Tewa pueblos that once thrived along the upper Río Grande.

The creation story of the Zuni was equally enlightening, and perhaps even more mystifying to ethnographers attempting to translate and understand it. Called "Talk Concerning the First Beginning," it was recorded by non-Indians on at least four different occasions. But during the first efforts, ethnographers relied on their own idioms and beliefs to interpret what could not be told by anyone other than a Zuni Bow Priest. The version most faithful to the Zuni language was recorded by ethnographer Ruth B. Bunzel. The telling proves— and this is undoubtedly true for all Native Americans—that the creation stories can be told only by medicine men, shamans, and high priests through ceremony and fully understood only by people of a common culture and language. The title of the Zuni creation story *Tcimikäna' kona Pe'na·we* ("First Beginning According to Words") addresses this point:

> truly this world, not anyone who
> very sun coming out, very goes in
> not anyone early, prayer meal (not) bringing
> not anyone, prayer stick (not) bringing
> very place lonely, his children both to
> thus to them saying, "you fourth womb to shall go"

Though the language and creation stories of the Pueblo peoples differ, their histories tragically converged with the arrival of the Spaniards in 1539. Estebán, a slave from the Barbary Coast, entered the Zuni pueblo of Hawikku in advance of Franciscan Padre Marcos de Niza; some historians speculate that Estebán must have mistreated the Zuni, because they killed him, and de Niza fled back to Mexico claiming he had discovered the fabled Seven Cities of Gold. Conquistador Francisco Vásquez de Coronado returned on July 7, 1540, with 300 men and vanquished Hawikku, avenging Estebán's death, before continuing his quest for the golden cities of Cíbola.

Norman "Buffalo" Lansin of Arboles, Colorado, is a Southern Ute artist born to the Weeminuche band.

The conquistadors who followed Coronado's trail north to the Pueblos treated the people even more savagely. Seeking revenge for his brother's death, the conquistador Vicente de Zaldívar laid siege to the fortress-like Pueblo of Ácoma on January 23, 1599; by finding a secret back way up Ácoma's nearly impenetrable position, de Zaldívar and his men overran Ácoma and murdered 800 Keresans. De Zaldívar punished the surviving adult men by chopping off one of their feet, and he kidnapped the young women for slaves.

The padres who accompanied the conquistadors were sent to ensure the peaceful settlement of New Mexico for the Spanish crown, but the padres called the sacred Pueblo beliefs and ceremonies witchcraft. As a result, soldiers burned sacred kivas and ceremonial objects, and jailed and tortured nearly fifty Pueblo religious elders in Santa Fe for practicing what the Spaniards called idolatry.

Under the spiritual guidance and direction of Popé, a San Juan Tewa, the Pueblos revolted, and in 1680 they miraculously turned the tide against their nemesis. The peace lasted a dozen years, but successive waves of colonialists, missionaries, and smallpox epidemics took a devastating toll on the Pueblo people, who were thought to number 33,000 before Estebán had entered Hawikku.

Despite such disastrous odds, despite the invading tide of California-bound immigrants during the 1850s, and despite the railroads that cut through the heart of Pueblo country in 1881, Pueblo peoples almost to every man, woman, and child would not give up their sacred religious beliefs and ceremonial practices.

There are only nineteen officially recognized Pueblos today, but nowhere else in the Southwest are the ceremonies as vibrant, colorful, and diverse. Here in the redrock country of New Mexico, the San Juan Tewa join the Zuni and the Keresan, the Aztec and Totonaca of Mexico, and the Northern and Southern Plains people for the greatest intertribal celebration of Native American cultural survival and spirit in the Southwest. Here, on the road of emergence, the lightning still flashes, the rain waters still fall, and the Pueblo people still blossom.

Cellición Traditional Zuni dancers of
Zuni, New Mexico.

San Fidel elder Bellamino is the leader and
traditional singer for the Pueblo Enchantment
dancers. (Redrock, New Mexico)

Pueblo Enchantment dancers Amoré Enciso,
Amura Enciso, and Erin Juanico of
San Fidel, New Mexico.

San Juan Tewa One-Horned Buffalo dancers.
(Redrock, New Mexico)

OPPOSITE: *In a Plains-style teepee, the San Juan Tewa elder Robert Aquino paints the face of a One-Horned Buffalo dancer.*
(Redrock, New Mexico)

Ashleigh B. Yamutewa waits her turn to
dance with the Zuni Olla maidens.
(Redrock, New Mexico)

Zuni Olla maidens. (Redrock, New Mexico)

Aztecas *from Mexico perform the* Huitzotochli, *"Left-hand Hummingbird Dance," at the annual Intertribal Indian Ceremonial in Redrock, New Mexico.*

Totonacas *travel from as far south as Veracruz,*
Mexico, to perform the ancient Zochiquetzal,
"dance of the quetzal."

San Juan Tewa Eagle dancers perform in downtown
Gallup, New Mexico, during the Seventy-Fourth
Annual Intertribal Ceremonial Parade.

OPPOSITE: Aztecas *from Mexico dance the* Huitzotochli.

San Juan Tewa Buffalo dancer.

(Redrock, New Mexico)

Hopi Corn dancers give thanks for a good harvest.
(Redrock, New Mexico)

In the depths of the Grand Canyon, Havasupai
boatman and musician Kirby Suathojame plays
reggae music learned from visiting Jamaicans.
(Arizona)

BIBLIOGRAPHY

GENERAL

Annerino, John. *Adventuring in Arizona,* revised. San Francisco: Sierra Club Books, 1996.

Annerino, John (photographs by the author). *The Wild Country of Mexico/La tierra salvaje de México.* San Francisco: Sierra Club Books, 1994.

Annerino, John (photographs by the author). *Canyons of the Southwest.* San Francisco: Sierra Club Books, 1993.

Annerino, John (photographs by the author). *High Risk Photography.* Helena, Mont.: American & World Geographic Publishing, 1991.

Annerino, John (photographs by Christine Keith). *Running Wild: Through the Grand Canyon, On the Ancient Path.* Tucson: Harbinger House, 1992.

Brown, Dee. *Bury My Heart at Wounded Knee.* New York: Holt, Rinehart, and Winston, 1970.

Confederation of American Indians, comp. *Indian Reservations: A State and Federal Handbook.* Jefferson, N.C.: McFarland & Company, 1986.

Curtis, Edward S. *The North American Indian: Being A Series of Volumes Picturing and Describing the Indians of the United States, and Alaska.* Cambridge, Mass.: The University Press, 1907–1930.

Deloria, Vine. *Custer Died for Your Sins.* New York: Avon, 1969.

Forbes, Jack D. *Religious Freedom and the Protection of Native American Places of Worship and Cemeteries.* Davis: *Native American Studies, Tecumseh Center,* University of California, 1977.

Gaede, Marnie Walker, ed., (photographs by Marc Gaede). *Bordertowns.* La Cañada, Calif.: Chaco Press, 1988.

Henry, Jeanette, Vine Deloria, Jr., M. Scott Momaday, Bea Medicine, and Alfonso Ortíz, eds. *Indian Voices: The First Convocation of American Indian Scholars.* San Francisco: The Indian Historian Press, 1970.

Hirschfelder, Arlene, and Martha Kreipe de Montaño. *The Native American Almanac.* New York: Prentice Hall, 1993.

Means, Russell. *Where White Men Fear to Tread.* New York: St. Martin's Press, 1995.

Powers, William K. "The Indian Hobbyist Movement in North America." *Handbook of North American Indians, Vol. 4: History of Indian–White Relations.* Washington, D.C.: Smithsonian Institution, 1988.

INTRODUCTION

Cooke, Sherburne F. "Historical Demography." *Handbook of North American Indians, Vol. 8: California.* Washington, D.C.: Smithsonian Institution, 1978.

Di Peso, Charles C. "Prehistory: O'otam." *Handbook of North American Indians, Vol. 9: Southwest.* Washington, D.C.: Smithsonian Institution, 1979.

Di Peso, Charles C. "Prehistory: Southern Periphery," [northwest Mexico]. *Handbook of North American Indians, Vol. 9: Southwest.* Washington, D.C.: Smithsonian Institution, 1979.

Fowler, Don D., and David B. Madsen. "Prehistory of the Southeastern Area," [Utah]. *Handbook of North American Indians, Vol. 11: Great Basin.* Washington, D.C.: Smithsonian Institution, 1986.

Martin, Paul S. "Prehistory: Mogollon." *Handbook of North American Indians, Vol. 9: Southwest.* Washington, D.C.: Smithsonian Institution, 1979.

McGuire, Randal H., and Michael B. Schiffer. *Hohokam and Patayan: Prehistory of Southwestern Arizona.* New York: Academic Press, 1982.

Plog, Fred. "Prehistory: Western Anasazi." *Handbook of North American Indians, Vol. 9: Southwest.* Washington, D.C.: Smithsonian Institution, 1979.

Rodgers, Malcolm. *Ancient Hunters of the Far West.* San Diego: Union-Tribune Publishing Co., 1966.

Schroeder, Albert H. "Prehistory: Hakataya." *Handbook of North American Indians, Vol. 9: Southwest.* Washington, D.C.: Smithsonian Institution, 1979.

Spicer, Edward H. *Cycles of Conquest: The Impact of Spain, Mexico, and the United States on the Indians of the Southwest: 1533–1960.* Tucson: University of Arizona Press, 1962.

1. PEOPLE OF THE MOUNTAINS: Apache/*Nde*

Ball, Eve, Nora Henn, and Lynda Sanchez. *Indeh: An Apache Odyssey.* Provo, Utah: Brigham Young University Press, 1980.

Basso, Keith. "The Gift of Changing Woman." Anthropological Papers No. 76, *Bureau of American Ethnology Bulletin* 196: 115–73. Washington, D.C.: U.S. Government Printing Office, 1966.

Basso, Keith H. "Western Apache." *Handbook of North American Indians, Vol. 10: Southwest.* Washington, D.C.: Smithsonian Institution, 1983.

Basso, Keith H., ed. *Western Apache Raiding and Warfare: From the Notes of Grenville Goodwin.* Tucson: University of Arizona Press, 1971.

Basso, Keith (illustrations by Vincent Craig). *Portraits of "The Whiteman."* London: Cambridge University Press, 1979.

Betzinez, Jason, and Wilbur Sturdevant Nye. *I Fought with Geronimo.* Harrisburg, Pa.: Stackpole Books, 1959.

Bourke, John G. "The Medicine Men of the Apache." *Bureau of Ethnology, Ninth Annual Report:* 451–596. Washington, D.C.: U.S. Government Printing Office, 1892.

Goddard, Pliny Earle. *Myths and Tales from the San Carlos Apache.* Anthropological Papers, Vol. 24 (pt. 1). New York: American Museum of Natural History, 1918.

Mails, Thomas E. (illustrations by the author). *The People Called Apache.* Englewood Cliffs, N.J.: A Rutledge Book/Prentice Hall, 1974.

Opler, Morris E. "Chiricahua Apache." *Handbook of North American Indians, Vol. 10: Southwest.* Washington, D.C.: Smithsonian Institution, 1983.

2. PEOPLE OF THE SIERRA: Mountain Pima/*O'ob*

Brugge, David M. "History, Huki, and Warfare—Some Random Data on the Lower Pima." *The Kiva* 26:4 (April 1961): 6–16.

Carmony, Neil B. *Onza! The Hunt for a Legendary Cat.* Silver City, N.M.: High-Lonesome Books, 1995.

Dunningan, Timothy. "Lower Pima." *Handbook of North American Indians, Vol. 10: Southwest.* Washington, D.C.: Smithsonian Institution, 1983.

Dunnigan, Timothy. "Subsistence and Reciprocity Patterns Among the Mountain Pimas of Sonora, Mexico." Ph.D. diss., Tucson: University of Arizona, 1970.

Faubert, J.B. Edmundo. "Los Indios Pimas de Sonora y Chihuahua." Manuscript, Arizona State Museum Library, Tucson, 1975.

Gentry, Howard S. "The Warihio Indians of Sonora-Chihuahua: An Ethnographic Survey." Anthropological Papers No. 65, *Bureau of American Ethnology Bulletin* 186. Washington, D.C.: 1963.

Lumholtz, Carl. *Unknown Mexico: A Record of Five Years Exploration Among the Tribes of the Western Sierra Madre.* London: Macmillan, 1903.

Pennington, Campbell W. *The Pima Bajo of Central Sonora, Mexico.* Salt Lake City: University of Utah Press, 1979.

Pennington, Campbell W., ed., and Baltasar Xavier Loaiza, *Vocabulario En La Lengua Nevome,* Vol. 2. Salt Lake City: University of Utah Press, 1979.

Sauer, Carl. "Aboriginal Population of Northwestern Mexico." *Ibero-Americana* 10. Berkeley, Calif., 1935.

3. PEOPLE OF THE DESERT: Pápago/*Tohono O'odham*

Bahr, Donald M. "Pima and Papago Social Organization." *Handbook of North American Indians, Vol. 10: Southwest.* Washington, D.C.: Smithsonian Institution, 1983.

Childs, Thomas (as written to Henry F. Dobyns). "Sketch of the Sand Indians." *The Kiva* 19:2–4. (Spring 1954): 27–39.

Chona (a Papago woman), and Ruth M. Underhill. *The Autobiography of a Papago Woman.* Menasha, Wis.: The Anthropological Association, 1936.

Fontana, Bernard L. "History of the Papago." *Handbook of North American Indians, Vol. 10: Southwest.* Washington, D.C.: Smithsonian Institution, 1983.

Hackenberg, Robert A. "Pima and Papago Ecological Adaptions." *Handbook of North American Indians, Vol. 10: Southwest.* Washington, D.C.: Smithsonian Institution, 1983.

Hayden, Julian D. "A Summary Prehistory and History of the Sierra Pinacate, Sonora." *American Antiquity* 32:3 (July 1967): 335–44.

Lumholtz, Carl. *New Trails in Mexico: An Account of One Year's Exploration in Northwestern Sonora, Mexico and Southwestern Arizona: 1909–1910.* New York: Charles Scribner's Sons, 1902.

Stewart, Kenneth M. "Southern Papago Salt Pilgrimage." *Masterkey* 39:3 (July–September 1965): 84–91.

Underhill, Ruth M. *Singing for Power: The Song Magic of the Papago Indians of Southern Arizona*. Berkeley: University of California Press, 1938.

Underhill, Ruth M. *Papago Indian Religion*. New York: Columbia University Press, 1946.

4. PEOPLE OF THE RIVERS: Pima/*Akimel O'odham*

Dobyns, Henry F. *The Pima-Maricopa*. New York: Chelsea House, 1989.

Ezell, Paul H. "History of the Pima." *Handbook of North American Indians, Vol. 10: Southwest*. Washington, D.C.: Smithsonian Institution, 1983.

Lloyd, J. William, ed., as told by Comalk-Hawk-Kih, "Thin Buckskin," and interpreted by Edward Hubert Wood. *Aw-Aw-Tam Indian Nights: Being the Myths and Legends of the Pimas of Arizona*. Westfield, N.J.: The Lloyd Group, 1911.

Russell, Frank. *The Pima Indians*. Twenty-Sixth Annual Report, Bureau of American Ethnology. Washington, D.C.: U.S. Government Printing Office, 1908.

Spier, Leslie. *Yuman Tribes of the Gila River*. New York: Cooper Square Publishers, 1970.

Mojave/*Makháv*

Coues, Elliott. *On the Trail of the Spanish Pioneer: The Diary and Itinerary of Francisco Garcés, 1775–1776*. New York: E.P. Harper, 1900.

Grey, Herman. *Tales from the Mohaves*. Norman: University of Oklahoma Press, 1970.

Kroeber, Alfred L. *Handbook of the Indians of California*. Bureau of American Ethnology Bulletin 78. Washington, D.C.: Smithsonian Institution, 1925.

Laird, Carobeth. *The Chemehuevis*. Banning, Ca.: Malki Museum Press, 1976.

Stewart, Kenneth M. "Mojave." *Handbook of North American Indians, Vol. 10: Southwest*. Washington, D.C.: Smithsonian Institution, 1983.

Hualapai/*Hwalapay*

Dobyns, Henry F., and Robert C. Euler. *The Walapai People*. Phoenix, Ariz.: Indian Tribal Series, 1976.

Hinton, Leanne, and Lucille J. Watahomigie, eds. *Spirit Mountain*. Tucson: Suntracks and University of Arizona Press, 1984.

Kelly, Isabel T., and Catherine S. Fowler. "Southern Paiute." *Handbook of North American Indians, Vol. 11: Great Basin*. Washington, D.C.: Smithsonian Institution, 1986.

McGuire, Thomas R. "Walapai." *Handbook of North American Indians, Vol. 10: Southwest*. Washington, D.C.: Smithsonian Institution, 1983.

Yavapai/*Pacə*

Gifford, Edward W. "The Southeastern Yavapai." *University of California Publications in American Archaeology and Ethnology*. 29 (3): 177–252.

Gifford, Edward W. "Northeastern and Western Yavapai." *University of California Publications in American Archaeology and Ethnology*. 34 (4): 247–354.

Khera, Sigrid, and Patricia S. Mariella. "Yavapai." *Handbook of North American Indians, Vol. 10: Southwest*. Washington, D.C.: Smithsonian Institution, 1983.

5. PEOPLE OF THE MESAS: Navajo/*Diné*

Brugge, David M. "Navajo Prehistory and History to 1850." *Handbook of North American Indians, Vol. 10: Southwest*. Washington, D.C.: Smithsonian Institution, 1983.

Gill, Sam D. "Navajo Views of Their Origin." *Handbook of North American Indians, Vol. 10: Southwest*. Washington, D.C.: Smithsonian Institution, 1983.

Klah, Hasteen. *Navajo Creation Myth: The Story of Emergence*. (Recorded by Mary C. Wheelwright.) Navajo Religion Series 1. Santa Fe, N.M.: Museum of Ceremonial Art, 1942.

Kluckhorn, Clyde, and Dorothea C. Leighton. *The Navajo*. Cambridge: Harvard University Press, 1946.

Luckert, Karl W. *Navajo Mountain and Rainbow Bridge Religion*. American Tribal Religion Series 1. Flagstaff: Museum of Northern Arizona Press, 1977.

Luckert, Karl W. *Coyoteway: A Navajo Holyway Healing Ceremonial*. (Translated by Johnny C. Cooke.) Flagstaff: University of Arizona Press and Museum of Northern Arizona Press, 1979.

U.S. Congress. *Indian Veterans*: Hearing Before the Select Committee on Indian Affairs. *101st Congress, 1st sess*. Oversight Hearings on Indian Affairs. November 14, 1989. Washington, D.C.: U.S. Government Printing Office, 1990.

Van Valkenburgh, Richard F. *Navajo Indians III: Navajo Sacred Places*. New York: Garland Publishing, 1974.

Van Valkenburgh, Richard F. *Diné Bikeyah, "The Navajo's Country."* Window Rock, Ariz.: Office of Indian Affairs, Navajo Service, 1941.

Watson, Edith L. *Navajo Sacred Places.* Window Rock, Ariz.: Navajoland Publications/Navajo Tribal Museum, 1964.

Wyman, Leland C. "Navajo Ceremonial System." *Handbook of North American Indians, Vol. 10: Southwest.* Washington, D.C.: Smithsonian Institution, 1983.

5. A GATHERING OF NATIONS

Zuni/ *Siwi*

Bunzel, Ruth L. "Introduction to Zuni Ceremonialism." Pp. 467–544 in the *47ᵗʰ Annual Report of the Bureau of American Ethnology for the Years 1929–1930.* Washington, D.C.: 1932.

Woodbury, Richard B. "Zuni Prehistory and History to 1850." *Handbook of North American Indians, Vol. 9: Southwest.* Washington, D.C.: Smithsonian Institution, 1979.

Ácoma Keresan/ *Ákumeca*

Garcia-Mason, Velma. "Acoma Pueblo." *Handbook of North American Indians, Vol. 9: Southwest.* Washington, D.C.: Smithsonian Institution, 1979.

Stirling, Matthew W. *Origin Myth of Acoma and Other Records.* Bureau of American Ethnology Bulletin 135. Washington, D.C.: 1942.

White, Leslie A. "The Acoma Indians." Pp. 17–92 in the *47ᵗʰ Annual Report of the Bureau of American Ethnology for the Years 1929–1930.* Washington, D.C.: 1932.

San Juan/ *Tewa*

Ortíz, Alfonso. "San Juan Pueblo." *Handbook of North American Indians, Vol. 9: Southwest.* Washington, D.C.: Smithsonian Institution, 1979.

Parsons, Elsie (Clews). *The Social Organization of the Tewa of New Mexico.* Memoirs of the American Anthropological Association 36. Menasha, Wis. 1929.

Other

Callaway, Donald G., Joel C. Janetski, and Omer C. Stewart. "Ute." *Handbook of North American Indians, Vol. 11: Great Basin.* Washington, D.C.: Smithsonian Institution, 1986.

Drake, Samuel G. *The Old Indian Chronicle.* Boston: Samuel A. Drake, 1867.

Hitten, Michael. *Wovoka and the Ghost Dance.* Carson City, Nev.: Yerington Paiute Tribe/Grace Danberg Foundation, 1990.

Wissler, Clark, "General Discussion of Shamanistic and Dancing Societies." *Anthropological Papers of the American Museum of Natural History* 11 (12): 855–76. 1916.